Ethics and the Modern Guru

Peoples   Temple   Edition

table of contents

editorial

Much has changed since the beginning when we first conceived of Ethics and the Modern Guru, so much so, that in many ways this can be seen as the first real issue. As often tends to be the case in life, things do not just fall in place, as rather one has to turn things around until it fits into a suitable space where it makes sense. As such, our aim is to as much as possible stand on our own legs and move to have our own trajectory moving within our own field.

One thing that has been contemplated is the name 'Ethics and the Modern Guru'. Some people get confused by the name, even to the extend where some think we are situated within the realm of gurudom and related Eastern mysticism. This however is not so, and it is definitely not the case that we seek to instill a different kind of spirituality or seek to cut a line between good gurus and bad gurus. As such it ought to be noted that we do not present anything that fits within the enlightenment business or the related businesses of coaching etc.

To explain a little further concerning the name; the word 'guru' is meant in a more open sense of everything imposing itself upon the individual, as having answers and being able to guide towards something higher or better. As for the word 'ethics', it is not meant entirely in the now common sense of the word, but rather in a more classical sense, where ethics means the character of our habitualities. As such, the reason we use the name 'Ethics and the Modern Guru' is a complex inquiring into the reasons why we seek something higher, and how rather easily we fall prey to the habits of others and imagine them as being this new exotic higher way of living.

Our aim is not so much to judge things (be they people or events), but rather to try and offer certain elucidation, whereby we may come to have some more clarity concerning such events. As such, we do not seek to deal in truths, give you a sense of comfort or take away your fears; no, we only seek to inquire and look a little deeper into things, and we present this for you to do with it whatever it is you wish.

As for the use of the word 'modern', there is no denying that we live in a day and age dominated by the concept of the information highway. Especially now when so many people are in possession of smartphones, information is literally available at our fingertips, which is quite the opposite of how the world used to be, when knowledge was a distant something and learning was available only to a select few. Yet in spite of the vast knowledge available to almost everyone (at least in the industrialized west), 'we' have not become that more knowledgeable, and sometimes it even seems as if things are moving backwards instead.

The use of the word 'modern' refers to both 'ethics' and 'guru'. At moments our modernity has us running scared; there is so much information out there, that we feel threatened because of the growing dissonance between our habituality and possible new paradigms and configurations. The information highway presents us with all this new knowledge threatening the dominance of our habituality, and it is here that we also find the birth of the modern guru, this person or event promising this new habituality, whereby all the anxiety caused by modernism shall be taken away.

So in a way the concept of modernity is central to our decision to use the name 'Ethics and the Modern Guru', since everything we inquire into is mainly situated within it. This is especially evident in this publication, as it deals with one of the most horrifying socio-spiritual events ever, namely the rise of The Peoples Temple and the unfortunate culmination in the Jonestown massacre. What many may neglect however, is that this event is not simply something that took place (as some may be inclined to think) at the fringes of society. In other words, the tragic fate that has befallen on those who died, those who survived, those who got out and the affected family members and acquaintances etc., is not just something isolated to those people.

The Jonestown event is something belonging to the whole of man and as such it is something that happened to all of man. This event is part of our crisis of modernity, and it is this we seek to address, because whether we like it or not (or dare to admit to or not) we all stand at the exact same spot and are faced with the same 'anxieties' as we move further into a future unknown. Regardless of how we relate to society, we all are confronted by it, the only difference lies in how we deal with things and whether or not we can deal with the ever increasing bombardment of information.

No one is ever truly free from anxiety, and hence to a certain measure we all our prone to being manipulated. The best remedy against this is to think, but this is never as easy as it sounds, because we often confuse thinking with a mere stream of thoughts or with opining. It is often easy for 'gurus' to hijack our minds and fill it with their thoughts and make us imagine we are thinking for ourselves, as such we must always be willing to think even deeper and ask the question: am I really thinking? More importantly why do I think something? Is it because it is truthful, or merely because it offers comfort?

an introduction to
The Peoples Temple

When we first conceived of doing something concerning Jim Jones and The Peoples Temple we were met with certain skepticism, not because people doubt the horror of it, but because for some reason it is imagined as something that is in the past and that there are more important things to talk about. Obviously we do not agree with such an assessment, as we consider everything that happened concerning The Peoples Temple to be still very actual.

One of the most common mistakes people make, is to imagine The Peoples Temple was a typical cult that involved stereotypical cult members, this however is far from the truth. There really was little stereotypical when it came to The Peoples Temple, and rather than being setup as a cult, it is more of a case that it evolved into it. More importantly, a lot of the people attracted to The Peoples Temple were not at all the kind of people you would describe as lost, and hence became mixed up with a cult.

There are indeed cults and groups out there that teach rather weird stuff, and prey on people of a rather dubious mindset and intelligence. Indeed, this has almost become synonymous with our understanding of cults, namely the mistaken notion that it must be something outlandish and as long as we are relatively sane, we cannot become trapped in something like that. Nothing, however, is further from the truth, and that is why the story of The Peoples Temple is so important.

One of the most important things to begin with, is that unlike as found in many people drawn to Eastern Mysticism, where we find there is a certain movement away from life and society, the people drawn to

Jim Jones were drawn to social life. Many of the people were drawn in by social principles rather than through something mystical. So that must be kept in mind, especially since one must see the whole picture, and not just the later Jonestown development.

Also, as has been recounted by people who were part of it, one must understand the times of turmoil in which all this took place, which was the time of the Vietnam war and the USA's anti-Communist agenda, which tended to see all Socialist acts as being Un-American. It also ought to be noted, this was a time when racial segregation was still practiced; incidentally, the year in which The Peoples Temple was founded (1955) is also the year Rosa Parks was arrested for refusing to surrender her seat to a white man, and the beginning of the Vietnam War.

Though The Peoples Temple is categorized as a New Religious Movement, and especially in the early days there was a strong religious message as well, The Peoples Temple is somewhat different, since the main drive did seem to be social work rather than spiritual service, though Jim Jones did always enjoy to present himself as a Christ-like figure. More importantly, a lot of the people attracted to The Peoples Temple, were people desiring a better society, rather than people seeking a spiritual experience.

Nothing is more of a misunderstanding, than to imagine people within The Peoples Temple were mindless cult members, as a lot of them were probably more mindful than common man, especially the ones who would critique these people as being mindless. Regardless of where one stands on the political spectrum, or how one feels about social activism, it must be understood that many of the people in The Peoples Temple were deeply involved with social issues, thought about things and sought to make an active change to our society. As such for many of the people who fell prey to Jim Jones, their only reason was that they cared!

As mentioned already, to understand The Peoples Temple one must understand the times in which it happened, however, this should not make us jump to the conclusion that hence it is an event isolated in time. The reason why we feel this issue is so important is because it also is timeless, because as long as there is society, there will be a societal problematic and hence not just another Peoples Temple, but also another Jonestown is always a possibility.

We should never be as lax and imagine that now we live in different times and things are stabile now etc., as such, it must be understood that every moment in time, we always feel that either we have reached society's goal or it is just around the corner. Few ever stand still at the fact that everything we hold dear can crumble just like that, and that our supposed modernity is largely a myth.

To anyone conscious enough of a world outside his own fishbowl island, it ought to be obvious that not everything is alright with this world and that in spite of advances in society, we still deal with a lot of the same problems of inequality, hate and prejudice, and often it even seems that our modernity only brings us closer to a total collapse. As such, in spite of The Peoples Temple being a product of its time, it could easily become a product of our time as well, hence the importance of trying to get a deeper understanding of it and why we continuously ought to educate ourselves on such matters.

One should also never just dismiss the power of a cult leader and the power of charisma. We all think we cannot ever fall for things and that we think for ourselves, yet everywhere people are quick to fall to political populism. We always feel as if we are in control, but this never means that we actually are so, or even when we are in control, it does not mean this cannot be taken away from us. All of us can fall prey to something, and for someone to imagine he cannot ever become a victim to manipulation, is to set yourself up to become an even easier prey.

It also ought to be noted, that Jonestown was a later development, which happened because it became clear society in the USA could not be changed in an easy and straightforward manner. It would be easy to think of Jonestown's formation as a running away, but in reality it was not that simple, and at its root lies a real faith in the possibility of a more perfect society. As such, the people who left everything behind and moved to Jonestown (near Port Kaituma, Guyana) should not be branded as naïve escapists, but rather as people who ardently believed in the building of a more perfect society.

It is easy to imagine cult leaders as these crazy types of a person, who talk weird and it is obvious all is nonsense. Of course there may be cult leaders like this, but as always we should not fall into stereotyping things, as this also makes it easier for one to become indoctrinated. As such, it must always be remembered that it always is very easy to talk about things after the event.

That we now imagine The Peoples Temple events are of the past and that this could never happen again because now we 'know' etc., comes to show just how important it is we keep on being aware of this, as nothing is further from the truth, as the self-certain arrogance whereby some dismiss Jonestown as a mere isolated even in the past.

Though The Peoples Temple Agricultural Project (formal name for Jonestown) was a deliberate moving away from mainstream society, it ought to be realized that it still was something functioning upon the idea of society. As such, we should not just think of it as something marginal, as what drove the project was a new iteration of society. The thought behind it all, was that mainstream society is bad and that it just keeps on repeating the same errors and prejudices, hence Jonestown was meant as a new model of repetition.

Here it must also be remembered, that in spite of Jim Jones' Messianic tendencies, what drove The Peoples Temple was not so much something esoteric or even spiritual, as the main focus was social work. This concept of social work, and the need for societal transformation is important, because social unrest is always with us. It is rather doubtful that a perfect society is possible, especially since it seems rather improbable as well. Societal discourse drives almost everything, one only needs to look at politics for this, whenever there are elections, large parts of the political discourse concerns society. There always are people discontent with society and hence there always are people offering the promise of something new or greater.

It is easy to imagine we are above the possibility of manipulation, but it is always dangerous to think as such, as it means we become prone to dropping our guard. An important document in this respect is the Jonestown Death Tape (audio copies and transcripts can be found here: http://jonestown.sdsu.edu/?page_id=29084), where we find a rather calm Jim Jones coaxing the people into what he called "revolutionary suicide". One of the things Jim Jones says is: Have I ever lied to you? And indeed, as can be learned from survivors, Jim Jones was often benevolent, and that is of course how he managed to manipulate so much.

Benevolence can be a dangerous thing, and of this we must be extra aware, as it is easy to become a pawn through acts of perceived kindness. Manipulation can come in many forms, and one of those is by acting as a benevolent agent, which is how Jim Jones amassed so much control over his followers. Even if Jim Jones was always obsessed with power, it was not in an obvious sense, because he always presented himself as this direct social activist and acted against crooked social norms, both publicly and privately.

Attempting to bring this introduction to a close, if we have stressed that we must understand the historical settings that gave rise to The Peoples Temple and the Jonestown tragedy, then this is because it is not something isolated in the past. It is not just that another Jonestown is always possible, but rather that we always must remain vigilant against those attempting to use basic goodwill and social activism as a tool of manipulation, and use it in order to bend people to their will.

More than likely there will always be elements of social unrest, and it is good we remain aware of this, since the way many cults tend to operate, is through the promise of this or that utopia. It is good that we are socially aware and that we care about the needs of others, however, we must always keep things in check and ensure that we do not fall prey to ulterior motives and that our social idealism is kept in check. It is very easy for our minds to become hijacked through our own idealism, and indeed, this is generally the way cults and malicious individuals get us to join or otherwise do their bidding.

As a final word, the Jonestown event has become famous for the terminology of *drinking the Kool-Aid*, however, I find it is better that we do not read too much in such a saying, as to a large extent, it is something we are all guilty of. As such, on a closing note, I would like to point out that real people died here and that these people were not necessarily blind cultists. These people were victims and, more importantly, humans like us all. We should honor and treasure their memories and even their idealism, because the reason why many a person got caught up in The Peoples Temple, is simply because they cared, and this is how we should remember both victims and survivors, as people who care!

an interview with
David Parker Wise

Ethics and the Modern Guru:

Thank you for speaking with us on this important topic! I think what we want to know first, is who you are, and how you came across meeting Jim Jones.

David Parker Wise:

My name is David Parker, but I am from a split home. My stepfather's name was Wise and by time I left high school, I was going by David Wise. The custody battle between my father and mother, did not end there, and so I eventually wound up taking my name Parker back. At the time I ran into The Peoples Temple, I was going by the name of David Wise, because that is the name I had in high school.

When I left Texas, primarily because the thinking was far too narrow, it was at a critical time in American history. There was conflict over the Vietnam War, the battle between sons and daughters, and their parents; there was a generational battle taking place over the Vietnam War, where a lot of the older World War II people were not just prejudiced towards those opposing the Vietnam War, but were prejudiced even to the longer hair and cultural changes. There was this massive conflict in homes all across America, and so I left Texas. At that time, I was looking for ways to fulfill the reasons why I was born and find out where I was at. There was a narrow minded environment in the panhandle of Texas, and so now I live in Austin, Texas; which is as if it is not even in Texas, and is considered to be more like San Francisco. The attitude to keep "Austin weird" is a slogan on t-shirts, it is a big pot smoking city, with musicians and artists, and that sort of thing.

The panhandle was known for what people coined as being a bit more redneck. So I traveled to California, and was checking out religions and every kind of group there was, looking for any group in the world that looked like, and was involved in 'the truth'. From my view of the truth, at that time, I especially appreciated what, later on, Jim Jones coined as 'Apostolic Socialism'. The idea increased humanitarianism; human service type of priorities were not on the top of the list in society at the time, nor are they during current modern times now. Later I learned of Jim Jones' notion, that Socialism or Communism is somewhat validated in religion as Apostolic Socialism. In other words, on the day of Pentecost, they went house to house, let us have a quotation from Karl Marx, "from each according to their ability, from each according to their need", this is a direct Marxist quotation, but it is also a direct biblical quotation; so the idea that government was to restrict religion and stay out of politics, is a way to control the people, and Jim Jones was recognizably crossing over those barriers, implying that parts of the bible, like to feed the hungry and clothe the naked, were in principle the true definition of religion, as we should define it, as love and to manifest that love in the world around us. So this was a very compelling message for a young man trying to define a religious purpose, or instead of religious, let us say a spiritual purpose.

So in the beginning then, I saw eye to eye with their philosophy and was very impressed by it. I met all of the people in the San Francisco area Peoples Temple first, and then traveled up and lived in the Ukiah area, where I was a part of the entire original group that at that time was not considered to be crazy or anything like it. At that point Jim Jones was not considered to be crazy; now there are points where people can be eccentric in their personality, but maybe that is just common for all people. But when later on he became involved with amphetamines, Jim Jones went over the top, so whatever seeds of instability he had inside of him, became overwhelming in the presence of substance abuse.

At that time then, a division was created, between his schizophrenic behavior and paranoia, and my belief that I did not want to go along with any wrong doings. Such as, I was opposed to public spankings and things that seemed to be wrong, like: intimidating or bullying people and indirection, as well as doing things sneakily, like bullying in order to acquire property, instead of it being purely voluntary. I was against any form of manipulation and such things, and this opposition resulted in me leaving in 1976, when more and more Jim Jones was on the road to his destruction, though I did not imagine for it to be a destruction of all the people, as a mass murder. That is a separate subject of great interest. To stick with the thought-stream I am on, I got away from Jim Jones and then found there was a contract hit on my life. He hunted me down twice and found me twice, so it was quite a difficult thing to actually get away from.

While with The Peoples Temple, I had become a pastor of my own Los Angeles church and during that time period I only saw Jim Jones about once every two weeks. So people, who would like to say, "why would you be around someone crazy like that, you must have been a cult member or whatever", no, it was quite sincere and open when I first arrived in Ukiah and joined the college crew. I knew everybody. I can truly speak about historic incidents that other people may not know about, and knew Jim's people, in their dormitories there, of the Santa Rosa Jr college. I wasn't around Jim Jones there, but then was sent to set up a branch in Los Angeles. It was considered that I was amongst the most dedicated and what this means, is just that I really believed in human service and was not lazy. It was perceived that I was smart enough and all such kind of things. So as a young man I had the offer to be in charge of this very large church.

Looking back, to prove my point and address if I was a cult member of Jim Jones; I had a respectful relationship with him, only seeing him once every two weeks, when he came down from Ukiah and San Francisco for Saturday and Sunday only. For four years, I saw him as the sincerest guy I ever met. Far humbler than anyone else. Later on, I went to San Francisco on the premise that "we need your honesty" as if they realized they were falling out from the original sincerity, and they wanted that; when I was asked to go to the original planning meetings, however, suddenly my honesty was not welcome. It was just a very manipulative environment, and I knew I had to get away from this group, as it completely transformed.

Jim Jones was walking along, enjoying the adulation of people calling him father. The meetings with the sixty people that were in the planning commission were constructed around a tremendous amount of egocentric games and manipulation, and actual honesty was not welcome. I stayed very quiet and of course appeared somewhat introverted. I was not interested in going head to head or toe to toe with Jim Jones, as he was employing a methodology that was just unacceptable to anyone, he might send thugs in the night, or whatever. I knew these people being sent, and so no one really dared to do anything to me. He sent Paul and Norman and a Jean Brown to Denver, and they just attacked me from behind. Paul tore off my shirt, I defended myself but before they left, one of them had a message, that Jim Jones had a contract hit on my life. The games were too syrupy, heady and hopeless. Hopelessly lost. Jim generated too much of a cult of power and manipulation. Jim Jones just copied cult tactics really well, really creative.

Ethics and the Modern Guru:

When did you see that shift in him harden?

David Parker Wise:

I wrote before in an article, that I believe it had all to do with the regular use of amphetamines. I think he had a proclivity towards paranoid schizophrenia and the amphetamines took him over the top. He would have been fine had he not used them, even if he drank alcohol and just acted like a nut. He began taking them early on, but it did not affect him until he took them awhile. Somewhere around 1972, he began to experiment more. If you look back at the man called Father Divine, well, he became old, and Jim Jones thought: I can get ahold of this movement and get all these people from the Father Divine movement. He had admired this four-foot little man; so you are looking at a guy that people used to call God (Father Divine) which is okay, all the Eastern religious people do that too. But Jim Jones used the bait and switch. He would say stuff like "Jesus said you are all Gods and until you realize that, I will just be God for you" and "I am almighty God". So now he did a bait and switch from sort of a Buddhist-Vedic-Christian, to go from there, and then say "I am going to model God for you", and of course it is all just a head game. Amphetamines cause these type of delusions, that is what it does. He also played Humble Jim, like: I am going to get the mop out of your hand and I am going to mop the floor, I am going to show everyone how to be a man of the people and be Mister Humble Guy, I do not care if I got twenty million dollars saved up, I am not going to wear new rings, or have expensive things, I am just going to work like everybody else, I am really available to everybody, everyone can talk to me; so it went from this, to Jim trying to imitate Father Divine and for him to even want to do that, he went down the wrong road; he came to a fork in the road and took the wrong turn. When Jim decided to emulate Father Divine, he made the biggest mistake of his career, which pushed him towards a cult instead of towards the missing culture. So culture would be anything that lives through us, a cult would be anything that holds you down. When Jim was trying to introduce things society needed and he was a humble man, he would say: who is humbler than Jim Jones? Who is more accessible than Jim Jones? Who is more of a common average man than Jim Jones? He would say he was here for the message to feed the poor in our lives, and I thought this was great, that this man is great. Then he came to this fork in the road and came to think, as to how back in early Philadelphia Father Divine put together this big movement, and was feeding all the poor and had people donating all of this money, to him; all of this money, and he was the central figure, and Jim thought: ok, well I need to have that much control, I need to be like the President; and this of course is like a cult of personality. So Jim Jones decided to imitate, Father Divine. You got a four-foot guy, talking with a weird accent (Father Divine) saying he is God, that is more like an anomaly, almost like a tourist attraction; but if you get a white guy, walking around saying he is now God, you are going to get a completely different reaction. Everyone will get scared of what you are up too. No one was really threatened by Father Divine, but Jim Jones' attempt to pull this off did not really work.

His lust for power was the reason Jim tried to pull it off, but also his disdain, his disdain that nothing works, that people are all lying, and so he thought he needed some centralized control. So in the beginning, before he got on amphetamines, he did not actually believe that way. I remember the last conversation I had with him, where I said: "Jim, you used to believe that guilt was bad, and now you changed your entire beliefs, now you believe in using guilt to control people"; he answered: "some of us just, of course, use the standard method of skirting a confrontation, but some of us have found that guilt can be very useful", and I said "ok, I am not debating this with you Jim, but I am going on record that you completely changed your position, like from white to black." This is similar to when he was generating fear, and I remember when we met the last time, and he bragged that he tried to scam me about a couple of things right to my face afterwards. People that say Jim Jones raped them, that is not what I saw personally. I have no knowledge of it. This man did believe that anything he can get you to do, was okay. But if you stood up to him and said "I don't turn that way" he would say "I admire you for that" he would also hate you, but there was a part of him that admired you. Now to bring up sexuality, not that anything like that is important, he was bisexual and was molested by his father because of which he had a hatred for controlling men. He had some problems in the sexual area, control issues.

I also want to slip this in for added context. People ask how this could have happened, and so it is important to listen to my point, that Jim Jones says that whatever he can get you to do, is okay. So if somebody can get you, according to his concept that the end justifies the means, to be all things for the cause. The idea that if you could get people to do things, makes it all okay and lets you off the hook, that is the end justifies the means. You cannot just go killing people in the name of life. You cannot screw for virginity. He really did believe that it is okay if you can get someone else to do something. This is at the heart of understanding Jim Jones. He did not think he was ever wrong. Now, you can ask whether or not that is like Charles Manson, he also never put his hands on killing anybody, or if he is not like an organized crime boss. Even though they were influenced emotionally and psychologically, he thought all that was fair. He wanted these people to protest and die, and they voted to die. Who was in charge of stopping that? He is the last guy you want to insult in his insecure mania. I was on the radio and I was blocked and protested. One lawyer told Jim he was crazy, and he was drugged and died in a lock up.

Ethics and the Modern Guru:

So your relationship with some of survivors is not good? Are you in touch with Stephan Jones?

David Parker Wise:

Some of the survivors just do not want me to tell things they have done. I am a completely different kind of a person, no one can say I ever did one thing wrong with Jim, and I also stood up to him. I could have taken a million dollars from Jim, but I was not for sale at any price. Many of them were put in positions and many stayed out of the heat and went along with him. Stephan Jones is the only biological son of Jim Jones and has a respectful relationship towards me, and I respect him. He developed a hatred towards his father. I tried to show him more human sides to his father. You see, when somebody is bad or loses his mind or gets addicted to drugs, there is no sense in acting like society is perfect, but this is just a lone madman. Jim Jones was actually quite the charming and interesting person, until he became addicted. His attributes were overshadowed by repugnant behavior; it would make you want to barf. Ok, so his son, a very nice guy and a very smart guy, we have a lot of respect for one another; there is a long battle and he needed the balance of showing good things about his father, he had no power to resist his father, he was helpless. Jim Jones was an extraordinary copycat. He copied the tactics of our government and of the military and if anything, was doing it better than them. We do not find this acceptable and want to point our fingers as if he is a lone madman. When in fact he was becoming very successful, very fast. Using the wrong methods of a cult, monopoly controlled government and even the mafia; Jim loved to make people afraid. I had no interest in being a party or witnessing those things. I know quite a bit about everybody and they try to silence me. I am not going to make anybody look bad and there is no need to mention their names like that, unless it is really vital. There are enough people to talk about that are already dead. There are some power freaks that may have never learned their lessons and should have walked away when they did not. Jim trusted me like a sibling, trusted me to open up about different things. People envy you because you have something they do not. Some of the first people that will cut off your legs, are the people who were adoring you. They will cut you to pieces, if you were lying or were not true, so all of that devotion flips almost like murder. The biggest attackers are the ones who believed in you before, and so instead of seeing the reality behind Jim Jones, most of those who adored him before continue to live in hate. They were tricked, so many of these survivors are now involved in social change. Many are so burnt and bitter, once bitten, twice shy.

Ethics and the Modern Guru:

So there is a lot of self-shaming that is difficult to work through? How has this experience kept you from being bitter?

David Parker Wise:

That is really very important and you hit the nail on the head with this question. I was really motivated before I met Jim Jones. I was talking to a survivor and he said to me "but you already believed in all of this, before you met Jim Jones, you were a revolutionary and wanted to change the world when we met you!" That is true. Such a dramatic thing occurring, and a compelling desire in me, to show that it is not all hopeless. Not only did I want to naturally work for world improvement, I wanted to inform everyone that society is a cult. So instead of blaming individual adoration, we can see that he was a copy of it, this is how this is being done in the big picture of everyday life and we are children and pawns and do not know it. How many Jonestowns are there not in the millions of deaths caused by war and famine? Who do we have to protect us? Well that is all a cult. We have to recognize the cult that we are in and the cult that surrounds us. Jim Jones, under the pretense he was going against, copied and decided he wanted to be the enemy, more than he wanted to defeat the enemy. So the bait and switch was more against his own self. We have to look out, for where the manipulator becomes the manipulated by his own manipulations.

Ethics and the Modern Guru:

You have a website (http://www.freeenergyparty.org) What is your message?

David Parker Wise:

We formed the first legal political party (Free Energy Party) in world history, which tries to face the cult destruction of the petro-chemical monopoly. We introduce free energy and organic permaculture. The free energy party is to introduce a new paradigm, to find a new way. I am not trying to live in shadows of Jim Jones, and have turned down the opportunity to appear on Oprah. I am waiting for the opportunity to make the correct message. Not just to show up and be in the group of bashers.

Ethics and the Modern Guru:

It almost seems after speaking with you, that you are the real deal Jim Jones could not be, as if you were his reflection haunting him. You had that genuine idealism and humanity he wanted, yet was incapable of achieving.

David Parker Wise:

This is exactly what happened. In the big picture, I also want to say that Stephan Jones is a smart guy and a nice guy, I don't want to see him in a gathering of survivors. What are we meeting like that over? To hate and blame Jim, and it is like the Barnum circus, come see the survivors of the worst cult murders. Especially after some of them have tried to block me from talking. That is the opposite of Stephan Jones.

Ethics and the Modern Guru:

We first wanted to speak with Stephan Jones, but it was mutually withdrawn, we were concerned he would be harassed if he said anything someone disagreed with.

David Parker Wise:

We want to be sensitive to Stephan. Good for you. If he reads this, I want him to know that the chapter is coming in my book, it is a hard, hard, hard road. I did not want to come in on the Barnum and Bailey circus, and I could have shown up at survivor meeting and hugged everyone, but the protests against me, is too much. There is a reason Jim Jones had everyone do his work; when you disguise responsibility, when you hide the responsibility amongst a bunch of people, nobody did it. Basically in a cult people go along and do not feel like they did it. All of us did this! You have to walk away! The night before people drank the poison, some people said "fuck this" and took off, not caring what the dangers were, they got away. I was not thrilled going in the climate of survivors. I feel different.

Ethics and the Modern Guru:

Thank you.

an interview with
Laura Johnston Kohl

Ethics and the Modern Guru:

So great to be able to talk with you. We had the pleasure of reading your book, "Jonestown Survivor, an Insider's Look" and found it was an amazing description of what led you to Jim Jones, and the subsequent journey of how you got out and where you are at today. I think it is very educational to understand the perspective of someone who lived through it, especially since people tend to think only certain personality types are attracted to a 'cult', and that is just not the case. As you established in your book, there is no such thing as someone who is prone towards a cult. Instead we get to know who you really are, the idealism you carried and the hopes and dreams. And how this wrapped up in The Peoples Temple. If we can go back to the beginning, and how you first got involved, especially for those that have not read your book yet, if you can expand on that just a bit.

Laura Johnston Kohl:

I was born in Washington, DC; my mom was always a progressive, but kind of a closet progressive, because she had three daughters to raise on her own, so she had to be very careful, but she always had integrity and would never step back from standing up for what is right, but would not stand on street corners, like I. She was always a role model for me, and so we helped get John Kennedy

elected (in 1960) and she was so involved that she got tickets for the inaugural ball. She was an activist in the Democratic Party, and also PTA President of all of our schools. She was a role model to me, who always brought out the best in people, and so, when I was growing up in the 1950's (I was born in 1947) I grew up at a time when the civil rights movement was just gaining momentum, we always had segregation, that was part of our society and we were changing that. So it was a time of change in the United States, and then the 1960's hit, when I was in middle school and high school. All of a sudden, all my favorite leaders and people I respected were shot by the vigilantes. So in the decade of the 60's, unlike any other decade, before or since, John Kennedy, Bobby Kennedy, Martin Luther King, Malcolm X, were all shot and killed. We had all these idealists and role models in our society shot and killed.

And so, by the time I finished high school in 1965 and went to college, we got involved with the war in Vietnam. I was pretty much sick of vigilantes and money running our government, and so my decision at that time, was to not let the world be run by police, and so I knew I had to be an activist. I was not sure exactly where to start with that, I did protest the war in Vietnam and I did go the Pentagon and help exorcise the Pentagon, to get rid of the 'evil' residing there and stuff (laughs). Another thing that happened to me, as I was protesting the war in Vietnam down Fifth Avenue in New York, is that I got tear gassed! The borders are really out of control, our 'free' nation is out of control and trying to oppress people. All that had a significant effect on me, first of all, I knew if you were to be involved in politics, you cannot get into drugs, so in a way that assisted me in not taking the direction of drugs, which some of my friends got involved in. I did try everything under the sun, no question about it, but my heart was not in just pursuing my own creature comforts. But I had to try everything, and like I said so many times, whenever there is a path, if it is a straight path, then there is one that veers off, I always takes the one that veers off, even when it's obvious what is the right road (laughs).

I have to take the hard road! That was an important time for me forming who I was. I was not then and cannot now, just sit back and see inhumane treatment of other people. That is kind of my background, then I was in college in Connecticut, I was a philosophy major. I had met someone who I was very impressed with who was a philosophy major, so I thought maybe that is the way to go, because I was not really drawn to anything else in particular. So I worked in housing projects near my school as kind of a work study, I dropped out of college and got married briefly, for a blissful nine months. And then I thought: where am I going from here? So I got involved with the Black Panthers for six months and had several living in the apartment with me. We would have meetings in my kitchen, but it ended up not working out very well for me. So I moved from that and went to Woodstock. I thought maybe "free love" and "free drugs" would be the way and I could have a little more fun in life, but that did not work out either for me. That kind of culture did not draw me in, and so at that time my sister in San Francisco called me, we are very close, and she said: I am watching your life cycle down, in the last four or five years you made one lousy decision after another. Come out here and live with me in Haight Ashbury, California, and I will take care of you, and we will get you straightened out. In March 1970, I moved out of Connecticut to San Francisco and my sister, at that point, said she had friends in the legal field, because she worked for legal aid. They told her there is a minister up in Redwood Valley, who had a wonderfully integrated church, and it was an activist group, and he was involved in all kinds of things I would be interested in. So the very first Sunday I drove there, just north of San Francisco, and went to his church in Redwood Valley.

I found what I was looking for, which was a multi-denominational, totally integrated church. People of all ages, education, all kinds of backgrounds, just really a fascinating group. They were purists, conservatively dressed, no one was flirtatious, all the things that I had as part of my personality at the time.

Ethics and the Modern Guru:

Understanding these times of political unrest is very important. So this situation presented itself in such a unique way, that it fueled your activism and wanting to do good and change the world, not so unlike what we are going through today, except we have the internet now for activism and information. People perceive this tragedy as if you were all mindless robots, but it was a very unique cultural experience of wanting to improve the world. People say a Jim Jones can never rise again, as if he acted like a monster from the beginning, which he was not, as this is how he amassed so much money and support, through manipulation, charm, and selfless work. We really have to be careful in saying "this cannot happen again" because cults are everywhere nowadays.

Laura Johnston Kohl:

Jim Jones would speak in line with heroes of our day. Jim was in contact with the 'new heroes' of our age, like Angela Davis, and so he would bring these conversations up in our meetings. Busloads of people would come from San Francisco, he also taught at high schools and a lot of us went to that. We were coming from a small church that was just on the edge of growing, and so some of us were even in contact with a few that grew up in "that temple".

It was very much a small church family. Once we decided we wanted to expand and go to San Francisco, I think that is when major problems really began to happen. Jim was just in love with power. As he got into the place where he had political power, with local government officials, he lost track of the individuals in his meetings. I continued living in

Redwood Valley, a number of us did; we did not feel it was so different, because he knew us and when he saw us would say hello. Once he got into the cities he was more anonymous, so our picture was from that early time when we knew him. In a way that stopped us from seeing the decline. We had this picture that he was a wonderful person. We had seen him up close and personal for several years, and we did not really change our image of who he was. So we did not pick up on clues, that he was getting more ego driven through this political cloud he was developing.

Ethics and the Modern Guru:

So there was not one thing peculiar about Jim Jones even in his humble years?

Laura Johnston Kohl:

Always with Jim there is a public persona and a private persona, so no matter what he portrayed to the general population, in his own house he was a tyrant. He had a long time mistress, he was really almost a split personality, between his public persona and the way he handled himself in his house. He was always able to create this image of being caring and concerned and loving, but he was not that way to everybody. So it was not like he just turned overnight; there were signs really early on, that he wanted to have power over a lot of people. He was not a sex fiend (I am pretty sure he was not) though I do think he was a power fiend, and used sex with males and females to get people in compromised positions. He did everything he could to demean people so that they could not feel like they could stand up to him. He was a magician at that. He just had it down, but those of us who were one step removed, did not see it.

Ethics and the Modern Guru:

Your book is so important, as we walk in your shoes and get to feel how the climate was and the idealism present within people such as yourself.

Laura Johnston Kohl:

Thank you. Another part of when I went to Redwood Valley, that I think is significant, is how Jim was also gifted in finding people that were at those crossroads. I did not have people around me that were part of my daily life or a support group, and so that is when I saw Jim Jones. Many of the people who went to Peoples Temple, and who survived or people I knew, were at that same type of crossroads. I thought of Jim as a protector, and early on in Redwood Valley he actually did intercede. I had a boyfriend who lived in San Francisco and when I moved up to Redwood Valley he kind of kept me on the hook, but he had a wife who he was living with in San Francisco. So Jim stepped in and said: you know, okay Chris, it's time to make a decision, and you must pick one now, or we will dissolve this, this won't be going on. He did protect me when it did not alert anybody to his own lifestyle, to what was going on with him. He did protect people, he had that relationship with almost every family. Not every individual in Peoples Temple but with every family, he helped in some way, like getting someone out of juvenile hall or placed out of a foster home, writing letters to judges to get people off from probation, got some kids tutoring to bring up their grades or have academic support. It was not just that Jim Jones was the leader of this group, he was involved in every aspect. He really was a hands on manager of everything, not just money, but also in how to support people. He was such a genius that he could do that; so when people ask: why would over 900 people listen to Jim Jones? It was because he had done something for every family, so he convinced them he had their best interests at heart. That is why they would listen to him and follow his instructions. He had proven himself to each family, almost everyone had seen a doctor, seen a lawyer, got into a hospital, been cared for; he had taken care of all these things that built up this faith and trust in him as a person. So in the end, where people thought he had never done them wrong before, how could he be doing it now? He could not be doing it now. So people trusted him, even at the end when he was crazed.

Ethics and the Modern Guru:

This was a different climate, where in most situations you are doing everything for the leader, Jim Jones was hands on and pro-active.

Laura Johnston Kohl:

But see that was the difference with Jim's public persona, he was genuine, if you took a step back and looked at him, you would say: here is a humble guy, who is willing to take care of people around him. On the other hand, in his inner circle of secretaries and mistresses, they had to give everything. Everything! They were not allowed to voice their ideas, no boyfriends, everything was Jim-centered. So in his inner circle, everything was done for him. But there is the code of silence, like we see in some police departments. No one talked about that, so the people in the inner circle, their position with him was precarious. They had to be absolutely silent about anything that went on behind these closed doors.

Ethics and the Modern Guru:

It almost sounds like the mafia.

Laura Johnston Kohl:

That's exactly right.

Ethics and the Modern Guru:

There was an incident in your book, in which you describe how you had a relationship and were heavily disciplined for that. How did Jim Jones find out about that?

Laura Johnston Kohl:

I lived in California from 1970-1977 and worked at the welfare department. I also was on the planning commission in 1975, and we were in a drug infested neighborhood, so we started to talk about building a promised land and we found Guyana, which is in South America next to Venezuela. We said, here is a country with a socialist government and they speak English, it seemed like the perfect paradise. So the planning commission, about a hundred of us, went down there in 1975, and I loved it. We had differences of opinion, actually, survivors have a difference of opinion on every single thing. I loved it. The moment I got off the plane in Guyana and saw the children, the people, the tropics … everything that I saw, I loved. In March of 1977, so exactly seven years after I joined, Jim asked me to move to Guyana, and I would work in Georgetown (the capital) and pick up people at the airport, help with residency papers, insurance and things like that. I would fill the boat with supplies; the ride from Georgetown to Jonestown was 24 hours by boat (12 hours on the coastline and 12 hours on the internal rivers). My job was to fill our boats with replacement parts for machinery and food for the community. People who flew in would then go up on the boat. For about a year I stayed in Georgetown, though I made trips to Jonestown and filled the boat every 3-5 days. So I saw all the most beautiful parts of Guyana. I saw the pineapples and coconuts, but that was my job. Towards the end, I was doing all the purchasing, I was picking up maybe 15 people maybe several times a week, who flew into Georgetown airport, an hour from my house. I had the only car, so I was constantly picking up people.

I started a lightweight relationship with a man who offered to help pick up people. And then we had a date and we had sex. We came back and everyone in the house, all 50 people, saw me come in after relations and asked: Laura, did you have sex with that guy? And I said yeah, and so it got to Jim. I was in the public forum and he asked: how could you do this, and be disrespected by having an affair with a man in Georgetown? One person slapped me, and then I was put in the public services crew, which was like a work camp for people who did not do the right things. So I was on the public service crew for about two weeks. You had to eat less, shower less and sleep less; it was a boot camp setting. Then I was put in charge of the public services crew, and then I moved on. In Jonestown, which was good and bad, is that we had our own 'everything'; we had our own system of government, discipline and counseling. In a way it was good as we had a caliber of our friends, but was bad if the situation was too severe. We did have a pedophile in Jonestown and we thought we could just watch the person, and that did not work. When we should have thrown somebody out we did not. People who were unhappy, they should have just been let go. We had 900 people there, even when congressman Ryan came, he said I can tell by the people in your community that many love it here. At the most only 30 people wanted to leave with him, but that would have been one too many for Jim. So even the people who were leaving told congressman Ryan: I have to go with you, because no matter what Jim says, he is not going to let us go, he will never let us go. And that was absolutely true. If Jim says he is letting us go, don't believe it.

Ethics and the Modern Guru:

Did people escape from time to time? What was Jim Jones reaction, if so?

Laura Johnston Kohl:

He would not let one person leave, one person would have been too many. In a way, the saddest case is the one with Larry Layton, Larry's sister, Debra left (she wrote the book "Seductive Poison"). Debra left and she came back to the United States, she tried to alert people about things that were going on in Jonestown, she was in the inner circle, so she saw things the rest of us never saw. So she tried to alert people and went to congress, talked to people and so on. Once she left her brother was on the hotspot to prove his loyalty, and with his mother dying of cancer (to which she did succumb) Larry was there by himself with no other relatives, and his sister (Debra) was considered a traitor, so that was a hot topic. So Larry was in the position, in the last few days, that congressman Ryan was going to leave, and then ...

Everything was Jim's instruction! There is nobody that did anything spontaneously without Jim setting it up. There is nothing surprising, nothing unexpected, as Jim has a hand in everything. Everything happening in Jonestown was either set up by Jim or his personal secretary, and so Larry was set up to go the airstrip and do some shooting. He did not even shoot Ryan, though he did shoot at the airstrip and was the only person that served time in the United States, for conspiracy to kill a congressman. His sister (Debra) left and Jim made him feel responsible for all the ills of the community, putting Larry in a tough situation. Jim is very spiteful and did not want people to leave, and would do whatever it takes too prevent it. So not too many people escaped.

Ethics and the Modern Guru:

That remains the enigma, his hold on people and the subsequent loyalty. Your description from being there, really sheds a lot of light, allowing us to understand this better.

Laura Johnston Kohl:

Jim would target certain people. Not everybody could see it, it would be sporadic if you could not watch it carefully. He would be a master of knowing what everybody was doing. He would target those that saw his facade and those he could not trust too. The Layton family did get the raw end of all of that. They ended up being a scapegoat of everything that went on in Jonestown, because everybody else was dead.

Ethics and the Modern Guru:

I wanted to bring the events up to that unfortunate tragedy. Where you were, how you found out and how you recovered from a tragedy of such magnitude.

Laura Johnston Kohl:

I want to back track a little more and then forward, if that is okay. When I arrived in Jonestown, we worked every day. We worked Monday through Sunday without a day off, until Jim's wife Marceline came down. She got us together and said: people need a break, so let us do a Sunday afternoon off from now on. So starting then, we started taking a half day off. Most of us were so driven that we just found other things to be completely absorbed by, so it is not like anyone just laid around. We just got focused on something else we have been wanting to do. So we were building a cottage and were really busy and had to lay the electricity, and so it was a very busy time for all of us. So all of us thought, once we were settled and we had enough cottages and enough of everything, we then would be able to relax. We saw that as a couple of years out.

The people who were the least happy, were those that said they did not want to do this for several years. This is really hard work and there was too much to do, so even in the community there were pockets of people who were not happy and criticized that we were being so single minded to work. We did not talk about it. You could not talk about any dissent. You could not criticize Jim or the schedule. Everything was very carefully controlled. It was like the Gestapo, when children would hear their parents talk about things, the children would go and tell the teacher or somebody else and then the parents were held accountable. It was just like that in Jonestown. You could not talk about it, and because I loved Jonestown, people did not confide in me, so I had no clue about the people who were unhappy.

I would hear things from time to time in public meetings, but it did not apply to me because I was happy there. I had no intentions of ever leaving, so I was completely oblivious to this whole sub-conversation. So in 1978, in Guyana, Jim's dealing with all these things back at home in San Francisco, as he now was being investigated by the media. Jim had an excuse for everything though, but the media was asking: who is Jim Jones, and why does he have so much power with all our local and national leaders, when we do not even know about him, he has never been vetted, has never been investigated, nobody can say a bad word about him? Finally congressman Ryan from San Mateo said he was going to come check out Jonestown. He had just enough reports that he felt like he had to see it for himself. So all of that was happening in the summer of 1978. But most of us in Jonestown were just working really hard and were exhausted. So whatever Jim said, he may have said a lot, but we were trying to do our work, so he was talking to people already distracted and exhausted. So, whatever he did or did not say, in a way, was a moot point, because we could not absorb there was a crisis going on in San Francisco. He did talk about congressman Ryan wanting to come down, and said: you know this is our plot of land, we left the United States and they have no reason to come here, we are not part of the United States.

Congressman Ryan said: you know, these are my American citizens, and it is the responsibility of the United States government to see what is going on, even if it is a religious group. So congressman Ryan was sent to come and Jim knew it, but Jim and his small group of people got more and more paranoid. Jim was into drugs, he was paranoid from them, was mentally ill and felt personally shattered if you did not follow him all the way. So we were working hard, and Jim was not hands on in the community as much. Jim's keepers would only let him out when he was really coherent. So there would be days we did not see him, or just heard him on the loudspeaker.

So Jim called me in his cottage to give me my old job back, and he said: alright Laura, do you think I can trust you and you won't get caught in a relationship? And I said: yeah I am good; so he sent me back to Georgetown, and when I first came back I thought it was just a fluke, that I was saved from being in Jonestown that day. The person in charge of the Jonestown house was Sharon Amos, and I worked for her at the welfare department for several years and she became a good friend. She was part of Jim's inner circle. I think Sharon felt that if I was given a message to kill myself I would do it. I think he thought I was an easy touch and that if Sharon told me to do something I would follow the instruction. So I thought it was a fluke, but nothing was left to chance. He thought he would just send me to Georgetown because I would just follow the instruction. So Congressman Ryan came and he stopped by the house in Georgetown, and he shook our hands, then he went off to Jonestown. We had put on this wonderful performance for him and he loved it. Then when he stepped off the stage, people started handing the congressman notes. People also handed notes to the media and his entourage that read: help me, get me out of here, I want to leave. The next day congressman Ryan, and about twenty people, left to leave Jonestown and went to the airstrip; Jim sent a truckload of people with guns to the airstrip, in order to kill congressman Ryan and whoever else was with him.

All together five people were killed and a number of others were wounded. They came back to Jonestown and Jim had everyone at the pavilion and said: you are all co-conspirators with me to kill a congressman, so there is no way to go back, there is no way back to the United States, because we killed a congressman and things will never be the same, you don't have any money because you gave it to me, you don't have a house because you gave it to me, your relatives don't want to have anything to do with you, because you are coming back as felons; your children will be taken away when we get back, and put in foster care and horrible experiences will happen to them. He went on coercing people like this for an hour and a half, just talking and his nurses and secretaries were sitting on the side, where the kids were sitting and gave them the poison. They shot up the kids with syringes filled with poison, so that just took any choice away from the parent, when they saw that 20 or 30 feet away the children were given the poison and they were dying. So if there had been any chance … up until then … (Laura weeps) He had to do that, not only him, but his inner circle that knew the plan …

The cyanide was in Jonestown for at least six months, and there were about ten people who knew about the plan before that day. So with all that happening in Jonestown, someone calls on the radio and they call Georgetown, San Francisco and Los Angeles and announced: everybody in Jonestown is dead, it's now time for all of you to commit revolutionary suicide. So I was in Georgetown and I had the car and Sharon Amos got the call, the coded message to kill ourselves. She sent me across town to get the basketball team. Our basketball team was in town playing against another team, so Stephan Jones (Jim Jones' only biological child) and Jimmy Jones were there and some other people who were part of leadership, and so I went and got them and then came back, and Sharon met them in a back bedroom away from the rest of the fifty of us in the house. She told them she had gotten this message, and it was time to kill ourselves.

Stephan Jones who was just 19, said absolutely not! It's all over! Let me get out to Jonestown, I am going to stop it! You know you could not get out to Jonestown. It was too late. Too far. He got on the phone and said: DO NOT FOLLOW ANY INSTRUCTIONS YOU GET FROM JIM. He really did stop further suicides, he stopped everything. He said it is all over, we did not even know. Then the police came, Sharon had killed herself and her three children. Those four were killed. The rest of us were there, and that is the first we knew of anything that went on in Jonestown.

Ethics and the Modern Guru:

We emailed Stephan Jones a few times, but we never knew he had stopped further suicides, he never mentioned it.

Laura Johnston Kohl:

Stephan is a wonderful and thoughtful person, he probably thought "of course I would do that!"

Ethics and the Modern Guru:

You and David Parker Wise both gave us tremendous insight. When I mentioned we were doing an issue on Jonestown, there was a negative perspective, and it was very disheartening and made us feel this could certainly happen over and over again.

Laura Johnston Kohl:

I was in Grand Rapids last fall, and I was at a library of the University of Grass Valley State. While I was out after the event at the college, two different young women came up to me and said they had just gotten out of a cult, and it is not over. Even politicians rev up hate, so it makes people want to run too something that is hopeful.

Ethics and the Modern Guru:

It's not over. We think we are so electronically savvy because we can google people and everything, yet we still have the same vulnerabilities; we still have that idealism and forget there are a lot of predators out there.

Laura Johnston Kohl:

When all you hear is someone spewing hatred, you need some way to make a difference. To make it not overwhelm you. That is why I do this, I was not going to be run by bullies in the sixties and I am not going to be run off by bullies now. I am ready to make an impact and so I work a lot on immigration and civil liberties and humanitarian things. I am a Quaker and try to do a lot of things every day, and I am a teacher, I just retired but still speak all over the country, universities, and other venues. So I feel, we cannot stop now, things are as bad as ever, if not worse. So we have a big job in front of us, to stop this prejudice, stop the hate surrounding us. We cannot live like that.

Ethics and the Modern Guru:

We have made a big shift with this topic, from our humble beginning as a free newsletter. We also note how cultic influences are embedded on some many different levels in society.

Laura Johnston Kohl:

We need people to be courageous. It gives you the inspiration to be courageous when it is your time. It is not your time every day, but there are things that happen and you just have to take a stand. That kind of courage just reinforces itself when you see it in other people, I think. Stephan Jones is one of the most courageous people, he did really save a lot of lives. Two other things that I think are very important in regards to The Peoples Temple, if you have a child today, and your child says "I am going to join this", meaning this cult or this group, don't forget Peoples Temple, they were dedicated people that were tricked by a conman. So whatever it looks like, appearances are deceiving, you cannot tell a book by its cover, you cannot tell a person by their public persona, you have to do the litmus test, to see what is real. When The Peoples Temple was forming, there was no historical situation where there was a leader, a benevolent looking leader, who killed a thousand people.

So now you can refer people, not to forget Jim Jones, do not forget The Peoples Temple. Now that is a point of reference you can use when you are talking to people who are joining communities. Back then there was no such thing, so we could not reflect back. So part of the reason we were caught by surprise, is that it was the first time in history American citizens were led astray, and a thousand people died because of a leader. People do not get it and ask: how could you do that? Well we never heard of a situation gone wrong. We were the first ones and it is a very important lesson for many reasons, just to get an understanding. Our perspective is that we were here for the long term, we never had anything to fear from Jim. He was the one who inspired us to do our best work.

Ethics and the Modern Guru:

David Parker Wise gave us a good perspective and said Jim was simply a pastor and it all just started as a grass roots movement. He said Jim was humble and helped everybody. People nowadays hear of Jim Jones, but do not see the whole development, and forget it could happen again.

Laura Johnston Kohl:

The whole identity of a con man. All you see is what he wants you to see, as he leads you to the goal. Jim was always a conman and it was pretty apparent once we got to San Francisco. Looking back, I can see it all clearly, here is a red flag, here is another ... but at the time, the conman identity was not something I recognized and so I did not see through it. We were being conned all the time. Financially, Jim made us feel he was all about the message, but he was all about the power, and the message was nice too, but the power was what kept him going. And he did not want to share it, he would never share the glory of anything he did. He was never going to let anybody take over. There were things he did that were awesome early on, he would fight the powers that be, like adopt a black child. But I think power corrupted him absolutely. His trick knee: when he got the power, he abused it.

Ethics and the Modern Guru:

Not to mention the toxic combination of mental illness and drug abuse. Thank you so much for talking with us, and breaking down this tragedy so that we can all grasp the historical importance, and learn from it, thank you.

an interview with
Rebecca Moore

Rebecca Moore is the site manager of the website: Alternative Considerations of Jonestown and Peoples Temple (http://jonestown.sdsu.edu), which she founded together with her husband Fielding McGehee III, who serves as its research director.

Ethics and the Modern Guru:

Your website is one of the most complete resources concerning the Jonestown event, what motivated you to set this up, and what is it that continues to motivate you in making us understand this event?

Rebecca Moore:

We started the Alternative Considerations of Jonestown and Peoples Temple website in 1998, when I was teaching at the University of North Dakota. This was the twentieth anniversary of the deaths in Jonestown, and it seemed apparent that the news media had not learned anything in the two decades that had elapsed. Despite the fact that there had been a lot of scholarly attention paid to Jonestown and Peoples Temple, we were finding that reporters were interviewing the same individuals as they had in 1978, and that the narrative did not reveal any fresh viewpoints or voices. We wanted to provide an alternative to that, to include the voices of other survivors, and that is what we have been able to do in the "Personal Reflections" section of the website (http://jonestown.sdsu.edu/?page_id=16994).

Ethics and the Modern Guru:

What impresses us the most is your mission statement, and your determinacy to showcase the humanity of the victims. Do you think that the tendency to dehumanize people and label them as mere victims, is something because of which we ultimately may be more prone to become a victim ourselves?

Rebecca Moore:

Because the deaths were so horrifying people could not identify with the victims, and news reports that only showed corpses and bodies, exacerbated this problem. I think that if we fail to recognize ourselves in tragedies like this, if we fail to see that "it could have been me, I could have followed a charismatic leader," then we too may fall victim to anyone who sings the song we want to hear.

Ethics and the Modern Guru:

Researching Jonestown is a very tough task, the work you have done not only has taken up incredible amounts of time and energy, but I can imagine it also must be very hard emotionally, how do you deal with this?

Rebecca Moore:

I have had two reasons for pursuing the study of Jonestown and Peoples Temple. The first is personal: my two sisters and our nephew died in Jonestown on November 18, 1978. We have always wanted to find out what happened, since we could not believe they voluntarily took their own lives. But since Carolyn and Annie were true believers and were in the leadership group, they definitely killed themselves. The second reason is professional: I have been engaged in the academic study of New Religions for more than twenty-five years. I guess I have been able to compartmentalize my personal feelings from my scholarly endeavors pretty well. I do see the website as combining both the personal and the professional, by giving space for painfully honest reflections by survivors, along with academic analyses of the group and its leader. If my personal goal is to achieve some measure of justice or memorialization for those who died, my professional life has in many ways served that purpose.

Ethics and the Modern Guru:

As someone who has done so much research in this field, what are the lessons you have drawn from this for yourself?

Rebecca Moore:

The lessons I would draw are primarily:

1) We are all looking for a savior figure. Most of the time we are lucky, and don't find him or her! But we do seek leaders who tell us what we want to hear.

2) If a group lacks the ability to criticize itself, it is a dangerous group. I do not mean the ability to criticize individuals (which happened a great deal inside Peoples Temple), but the ability to criticize the group and the way it functions, particularly the leader. If it is not possible to change the leader or leadership without causing a major schism, that is problematic.

3) Related to this, is the ability to laugh about the foibles of the group and its leader. If we cannot poke fun at what we are doing, we have lost critical distance and have become vulnerable to the dictates of the group rather than to our individual conscience.

4) Finally, we need to listen to what our individual conscience is telling us. I have heard several survivors of Peoples Temple admit that they knew

what they were doing was wrong; but since everyone else was doing it, they believe it was expected. Moreover, they felt the end justified the means, so they could rationalize what they knew was wrong. If our conscience says "Wait a minute," we need to listen to it.

With all these lessons listed, I'm not sure that any have been taken to heart, especially by those involved in new religions.

Ethics and the Modern Guru:

A lot of the people who fell prey to The Peoples Temple, were deeply caring people who wanted their actions to have a lasting impact upon society. Knowing what happened, people may become even more numb to the realities of our social world and people preying upon our sense of benevolence. What would you say is essential in trying to balance said sense of benevolence, with the possible fear of such care going to waste due to unscrupulous people who are only into it for self-glory, and power etc.?

Rebecca Moore:

Our idealism does indeed make us vulnerable to unscrupulous people who may use our idealism against us or for their own ends. I think some of the lessons I noted above help us recognize a few problems to avoid. When people appeal to our good nature, we usually want to respond. We can observe leaders' behavior, however, to see if their own actions support what they are saying. In short, do they practice what they preach? If any group leader justifies a Rolls-Royce or a multi-million-dollar house and then asks for money to feed the poor, I would run like heck in the opposite direction.

Ethics and the Modern Guru:

Is there anything else you would like to say or comment upon?

Rebecca Moore:

One unexpected outcome of the Jonestown website is that it has enabled many survivors and family members to connect with others who were in The Peoples Temple but who were scattered after 1978. We did not foresee this possibility in 1998, but have only learned through the years that the list of those who died (http://jonestown.sdsu.edu/?page_id=33) is one of the most important parts of the website: maybe the most important part for family members.

Ethics and the Modern Guru:

Thank you very much.

the united states of jonestown

by Kathryn Barbour

Kathryn Barbour joined Peoples Temple in 1970, together with her companion, Richard Tropp, and they lived in the San Francisco Temple on November 18, 1978. Her essay "The United States of Jonestown" originally appeared in the 2013 Jonestown Report (http://jonestown.sdsu.edu/?page_id=40163) and has been re-edited by her for this edition of Ethics and the Modern Guru, a foreword has also been added by her. In spite of what happened, Kathryn Barbour has remained true to the principles that attracted her to The Peoples Temple and remains active in the field of social justice and change. She is the author of "Who Died on November 18, 1978 in the Jonestown, Guyana mass murder-suicides" (ISBN: 978-0692328132).

Foreword

A 2016 review of my article "The United States of Jonestown" shows its precepts holding. The only differences are that the pace has quickened, the powerlessness has deepened, and there is even less consciousness of our disastrous impetus. The media miasma has only thickened, despite people's uprisings of the last 3 years behind Silent No More, Black Lives Matter, and the Bernie Sanders campaign, which revealed the establishment juggernaut as only opposition can, though they did not slow its course.

Foreboding has deepened as well, whether expressed in the obsession with Planet X or the desperation spurring the drivers of this death march to keep everybody in line. With a revival of fears of nuclear holocaust, so long off our radar we can't even find it in the Memory Hole or remember when it was put to rest there, our scope expands to encompass Planet Jonestown.

Where's the recognition of our plight that I foresaw? Scarcely there, unless it be in this quote from Green Party Presidential Candidate Jill Stein, in an interview on the Ralph Nader Radio Hour on August 18th, in which she said:

> "We are not just going to go quietly into this dark night. In this election we are not just deciding what kind of a world we will be, but arguably, whether we will have a world or not going forward...I just want to note that 43 million young people in debt is enough to win a 3-way presidential race. So when they tell us that resistance is futile, that is the toxic Kool-aid, that is the propaganda that they're trying to use to keep people from self-mobilizing. And if there ever was a mobilizing entity, it is the Millenial Generation. We have the power to turn out and even win this race. Not just split the vote, but to flip the vote."

I approve of Dr. Stein's use of the Kool-aid metaphor here, and have spoken publicly in opposition to well-intentioned efforts to remove that phrase from public discourse, usually undertaken by supporters defending the honor of those who died in Jonestown. Its power is needed now more than ever, as a warning and a deterrent, to all of those in lockstep with Establishment dicta.

The United States of Jonestown

"Wise Men, as poor Dick says, learn by others' Harms; Fools scarcely by their own."
Benjamin Franklin, Poor Richard's Almanac, 1758

We are —increasingly— mirroring Jonestown in so many ways it is spooky. The correspondences now describe a near mirror image, except for a few marked disparities that are polar opposites. These inform rather than diminish the likeness. Both entities act/acted to groom their populations for an inglorious end. In considering them, I fear an impending plunge into the abyss.

In 1978 I was a member of Peoples Temple, living in the San Francisco Temple, a world away from Jonestown. Unlike those in Guyana, I ate well and slept comfortably. I knew I was missing the intensity and excitement of being in The Presence, but it was a relief I welcomed, though I would never have admitted it to anyone. After 1978, I considered myself as guilty as anyone in contributing to what happened, by my loyalty at all costs. The blinders were on. So for 35 years I've been determined not to let that happen again. But I'm still searching for the way to do it, that will Do It. All my efforts to date to counter the tailspin of this country appear to have only sped up the decline.

Let me make my case: We, the American people, are lining up and marching towards the figurative vat, or vats. And if we don't snap out of it, we may just take the world, as we know it, down with us.

We have come full circle, and the unthinkable is about to happen again. My obsession has been to understand the past so that future disaster may be averted, and in the process, to perceive the present as accurately as possible, trusting only my eyes and ears, and remembering everything. Over these years, by degrees so gradual, most have no idea it has happened, I've watched us fall in line with the final footsteps of my former family, those first-ever Kool-Aid drinkers, whose tumultuous passage on November 18, 1978 drew a sharp line of demarcation in our history, changing the game, creating the memory hole, issuing a blank slate to each of us, and commencing the rebirth and rearing of a nation of sheep. (Sheep have to be slaughtered sometime, don't they?) There would be another line of demarcation in 2001, the launch of the "War on Terror," and the one imminently approaching, the imperative to intervene in the Syrian civil war.

If I had to say where we are today, it would be that Vladimir Putin is the equivalent of Congressman Leo Ryan —that outsider trying to save US— and let's hope his frantic efforts for peace are successful, since there is a panic in Washington over how to respond to this unforeseen threat of a peaceful solution. Decision time is upon us. Will we drink the Kool-Aid or turn over the vat?

First, the similarities:

- Like Them, we fancy ourselves a world beyond and apart from the rest of humanity.

- Like Them, we live in a closed-circuit universe where an official narrative repeats endlessly and relentlessly;

- Although, like Them, we have critics, even strident ones, most are not aware of it, or if their cries are briefly heard, they are ascribed to base or devious motives, corruption or cowardice;

- Any remaining damage control or mop-up is accomplished by a tightly controlled PR team which makes sure such outbursts never reach the outside (or the inside), insofar as possible;

- Outside the bubble (where we cannot see), we are told the worst danger surrounds, awaits, and intends —nay, approaches!— to harm us;

- Within the bubble, our populations act to enforce the urgency of cohesion by ratting out traitors, intimidating critics, enforcing discipline and informing on each other;

- There is no safe haven from constant observation, interference, designs and demands in service to the interpreter of the One World inside the bubble, and his managers, who make sure it is the only reality, all the while telling us how free we are;

- It engulfs and compels through deft handlers who use flattery, condemnation, ostracism, and intimidation as carrots and sticks and, if these are not sufficient, drugs and deadly weapons, to enforce its dictates;

- All apparent divisions and distinctions are encompassed within the confines of the bubble, or else do not exist; and

- As with Them, resistance to the controlling power is futile. There is nowhere to hide, nowhere else to go. Exile? The very prospect is terrifying, entailing changes we can't imagine and risks we may well not survive. So there is no way but forward, one day at a time, one step after the other. As convinced of our individual powerlessness as we are of our strength in numbers, we helplessly defer to those who appear to be so sure they know. And just take the next step. And then the next. One more similarity I must add, since we are about to take the plunge:

- This horrific, disastrous end is so totally unnecessary, it is beyond tragic. It is criminal. What it is not is accidental.

The differences:

- Unlike the residents of Jonestown, we are well fed, replete with material comforts and except for the stubbornly stoical, either medicated or self-medicated to alleviate our stress or boredom or both, as applicable.

- Our politics are 180 degrees from theirs: selflessness vs. selfishness, revolutionary communism vs. capitalist monocracy.

- They were about a thousand people; we are a nation of 313 million.

- Our leader then was a man who said he was God. Our leader now is fronting, as did at least several presidents before him, for a shadowy overarching something (Corporatocracy; _____ [fill in the blank] _____ industrial complex; New World Order) or someone(s) unknown.

I won't try to chronicle the imperceptible degrees that took the US to where it is today. Indeed, the case I thought I would have to make has been made for me by this fall's events, and the resemblances of the US to Jonestown will I fear not be farfetched anymore by the time you read these words.

These last 35 years exist in a fog of competing assertions, constant revision and regular upheaval, as whole movements, struggles, wars and victories disappeared down the memory hole so quickly we're left wondering, did it really happen? Yet society itself seems static, even moribund, in the midst of a blur of technological, social and economic changes.

What has demonstrably, actually happened over this time? Public service, from the office of your U.S. Senator to your water treatment worker, has either become the province of the very rich and easily compromised, or been outsourced, so that anyone with integrity dare not enter the arena. We have watched the rise of the class society and its dual-track delivery of education, medical, and judicial services; we have to remind ourselves it was not always that way. Public airways are ruled by propagandists whose next targets are the few surviving newspapers, making them a "curiosity" only to be seen in high-end hotel lobbies.

As in 1978, I am a part of this society but removed from it. Not by physical distance as then, but philosophically. Like others, I'm immersed in the conditioning, but am mostly immune to its effects from long practice, making its dicta by now transparently obvious. That others may see things as I do must be the case, but until now there have only been hints, glimmers that this is so. No one captures the entirety of the situation, or sees the horror ahead. Nevertheless, I cannot suppress the hope —in fact, it is my only dream— that the reality I perceive will suddenly become clear and obvious to all as it is to me.

In order to avoid the unthinkable, we must 1) comprehend and accurately assess the status quo and 2) realize the power that is innate within us to change direction, in order to 3) avert the unthinkable outcome for which, as long as the spark of consciousness continues to flicker, we will never forgive ourselves.

1)   We are sleepwalking into oblivion, lulled by the measured steps of those around us to think we have no option but to do what we are (or aren't) doing. Risk-averse in the extreme, we relegate resistance to others and are encouraged in so doing the better to secure our possessions in insecure times.

2)   We do have the power to change the suicidal course of the US. It is the best-kept secret, it is ancient wisdom, and concealing it is the first objective of any propaganda: To make us unaware that there is another course and/or even if we disagree with the direction, convinced of our powerlessness to change it. This apathy is widespread today, but resistance on many fronts is also widespread in spite of every attempt to suppress it and hide the fact it ever happened. Consensus across many sectors already exists. What is needed is the will to galvanize realization, act in coordination, and address the problem.

3)   Once #2 is achieved, corrective action will be obvious. As befits a superpower, we can —and must— demonstrate leadership by abandoning the endless war in pursuit of higher goals, like actually setting an example for other nations in using our portion and no more of the earth's resources, while living lives richer in everything that matters. Sustainability, not growth, must be the new grail. We could do this by resettling our share of the world's refugees, studying their lifestyles, and learning from them how to best coexist on the shrinking earth.

The long work of healing the earth and humanity from the ravages of conflict, and restoring trust among its people will resurrect the hope for the future that we had in the last century. It was not the first casualty of the "War on Terror," but soon enough fell victim as the imperial juggernaut loosed wars of destabilization to cause pandemonium in the Middle East in order to control it and its resources.

Proceeding apace we shall be at the brink, facing the deadly draught before we know it. Whether we will be the "last, best hope of mankind" — or only the Last — may be what is at stake.

an afterword to

The People's Temple

As written in the introduction, we must remember victims and survivors as people who cared, this is not only respectful, it is also right. Nothing is more arrogant than to think these people were just mindless cultists, especially since the only mindlessness exists in dismissing these events as something that is just a cult thing.

It is always very easy to dismiss tragedy as something happening to others and to find a false sense of comfort in the thought that we could not ever be caught up in something like that. However, it also ought to be noted that cults are everywhere, perhaps not in the literal sense of the word, but rather that everywhere there are 'structures' commanding our attention and drawing us in.

It is also important that we do not fall into the trap of dehumanizing victims of cults, especially since a dehumanization of otherness is often a way through which cultish influence operates. The victims of Jonestown, as well as those who survived that terrible ordeal, were man in the same sense as you and I are man, and it is as such that we must remember them: as individuals belonging to the human species just as you and I do.

Finally, we would like to mention a great website that acts both as a tribute to victims and as a resource page: http://jonestown.sdsu.edu. This site is researched by Mr. Fielding McGehee III, and to finish this off I would like to offer a quote from the site, which is one of their main features: "Memorialization of those who died and those who survived the tragedy of 18 November 1978 in order to remember their lives and humanize their deaths."

an interview with
Benjamin Zablocki

Benjamin Zablocki is a sociologist whose main field of interest is religion, cults and the functions of brainwashing and charisma. The following 'interview' was done as a written questionnaire, and to respect the wishes of Mr. Zablocki, we would like to make the disclaimer that he is not a psychiatrist and that his words are a mixture of facts, opinions, theories and conjectures.  Furthermore, anyone who feels he is the victim of a cult or of brainwashing etc., should seek the help of well-trained and qualified professional such as a physician or psychotherapist.

Before beginning this interview, however, I would like to share a few notes of Mr. Zablocki, which he prepared for a lecture. These notes will help you understand Mr. Zablocki's research. For readability we shall weave these notes together in a single text, the words of Mr. Zablocki appear between quotation marks.

Brainwashing is "Not a metaphor!" but "An observable set of transactions between a totalistically structured group and an isolated member of that group with the goal of transforming that member into a deployable agent." Brainwashing is "A retail technique for retaining members, not a wholesale technique for obtaining members" and "has little or nothing to do with hypnotism".

"Under the right (i.e.: wrong) circumstances, anybody can be brainwashed", it "Requires initial enthusiastic compliance, a long period of uninterrupted time, isolation, totalistic control over the individual and the environment, and a supportive affectionate peer group." It is "a three stage process involving unlearning, new learning, emotional addiction to the group, and traumatic aversion to the forbidden and the sinful (...) it involves nothing more than plain vanilla techniques of influence that have been known to and studied by social psychologists for decades." Also, "Unlike hypnotism, brainwashing can get people to perform ego-dystonic acts (e.g.: in extreme cases has resulted in a parent beating his own child to death, suicide bombing, beheadings, berserker military action)"

The effects of brainwashing "Can last a lifetime with occasional reinforcement unless there is intervention." However, "With time and in the absence of reinforcement, effects are steadily (but slowly) diminished. Hypercredulity is the earliest to be diminished; implanted false memories often the last. With therapy, effects can be asymptotically extinguished but never 100% eliminated."

Ethics and the Modern Guru:

Thank you very much for speaking with us. How did you come to study brainwashing?

Benjamin Zablocki:

I started studying charismatic influence in isolated communal groups in 1963. At that time, more than a few people were becoming fanatical followers of charismatic leaders but I wasn't thinking about it in terms of brainwashing. I had read Robert Jay Lifton's book, "Thought Reform and the Psychology of Totalism" and was impressed with it but I thought of it as something Communist states did on a large scale rather than as something cults could or might want to do on a small scale. I did intensive participant observation field work in the Bruderhof (the subject of my first book, "The Joyful Community") and realized that what they did to their members corresponded almost exactly to each of Lifton's steps of the brainwashing process. I got to see the process in action at the Bruderhof and I got to see the longer term effects when I interviewed ex-members of the Bruderhof. Some of these ex-members I interviewed repeatedly over quite a few years. I feel it's important to say that my work at the Bruderhof was over 50 years ago and I have no idea whether they still practice any of these same techniques.

After the Bruderhof work, I taught at U.C. Berkeley and Cal Tech during the 60s and early 70s where my colleague, Philip Selznick introduced me to the key concept of "the deployable agent" in his lectures and in his book, "The Organizational Weapon." I received generous funding from the National Institute of Mental Health and the National Science Foundation and the Templeton Foundation to carry out a large scale study of 120 charismatic communitarian groups all around the country. Some results of this were reported in another of my books, "Alienation and Charisma". Work on that huge study is still going on, mostly by my students and former students. From the late 1990s on, I began looking at the long-term effects of people who reported being brainwashed in some of these groups. It's important to note that, of the thousands of members of these groups over the years, only a very small percent saw themselves as having been brainwashed and less than half of these fit the rigorous definition of brainwashing that I use. It would be a big mistake to think that every cult member has been brainwashed. True brainwashing is a terrible thing but it is fortunately not very commonly found even among cult members. To brainwash a person fully requires a big investment of resources and few cults will take the trouble to go through the whole brainwashing process except with cult members for which tight total control is deemed important. However, partial brainwashing is unfortunately more commonly found among cult members.

Ethics and the Modern Guru:

Why do you use the term brainwashing over other terms?

Benjamin Zablocki:

Please be aware that the use of the word brainwashing is controversial in the behavioral sciences and even those who use the term often vary in their definitions. Get people to define their terms. I don't really care what term people use as long as they define their terms carefully. As far as I'm concerned, it could just as well be called the XYZ process. Of the many terms that have been used in the literature, some are just curse words like mind control or mental rape. It's understandable that the victims are angry and want to lash out verbally, but these terms really have no scientific meaning. The two terms used more or less interchangeably by Lifton, "thought reform" and "brainwashing" are much more scientifically rigorous. I prefer brainwashing because I hypothesize that these are concrete changes that occur in the structure and function of the BRAIN (although not irreversible to anticipate one of your later questions) and also because the process involves not just thoughts. The manipulation of emotions is just as important as the manipulation of thoughts and one can't go very far without the other.

Ethics and the Modern Guru:

What is the difference between brainwashing and mass manipulation? And is this a strict difference, or do they involve the same neural processes?

Benjamin Zablocki:

Mass manipulation is a far more common process, easier to perform and easier to escape from. We're all subject to mass manipulation, at school, at work, on tv etc. More serious mass manipulation can happen in cults and political movements. It can be the prelude to making people vulnerable to brainwashing but it isn't in itself brainwashing. To put it another way, mass manipulation is a WHOLESALE way of OBTAINING followers. Brainwashing is a RETAIL way of RETAINING members and turning them into deployable agents. A mass-manipulated person may helplessly dance on his or her charismatic puppeteer's strings but a brainwashed person will do the charismatic leader's bidding even without the strings, even when the leader is thousands of miles away and has no way of directly spying on the victim. Unless the charismatic leader needs a person to become a fully deployable agent capable of such things as killing, smuggling, suicide bombing, or brainwashing other people, there is often no need for the guru to invest the time and effort needed to perform a full brainwashing.

Ethics and the Modern Guru:

What does brainwashing do to our (supposed) free will?

Benjamin Zablocki:

Brainwashing is a scientific concept. Free will is a philosophical concept. A scientific theory of brainwashing thus has nothing to say about the existence of free will. But one of the interesting (and diabolical) aspects of brainwashing is that a brainwashed person can become convinced that he is acting out of his own choices when he is really following his leader's orders. The reasons for this at the neurological level are not fully understood at this time and what is understood about it is quite complicated and technical.

Ethics and the Modern Guru:

So brainwashing is an individual thing rather than a group thing?

Benjamin Zablocki:

The popular perception that brainwashing is a group thing comes from confusing mass manipulation with brainwashing (see above). Brainwashing is (fortunately) difficult to accomplish. To brainwash a person is labor intensive and requires a highly controlled and isolated environment. Brainwashing is usually accomplished by focusing on one person at a time or sometime a few people at a time. Even in cults like the Manson Family, Jonestown or Heaven's Gate where most of the members were brainwashed, they were brainwashed as individuals or in small groups. Although mass meetings of brainwashed people can make the process smoother, faster and more effective.

Ethics and the Modern Guru:

What can make a person more (or less) prone to the effects of brainwashing?

Benjamin Zablocki:

Everybody is potentially susceptible to brainwashing including you and me. The real question should be what makes a person let themselves be put in the clutches of a brainwashing leader or group? And why, especially in the early stages where the brain is still fairly autonomous, why doesn't the person walk away once she realizes she is being brainwashed? The answer to this question would be long and rambling. It has to do with life-stage, with emotional vulnerability, the need for approval, the need to finding meaning in life, the need to self-medicate against anxiety, depression, psychosis and many other things. I'm certainly not saying that only crazy people let themselves be brainwashed; but sometimes, for people fighting mental illness, brainwashing can feel like just what the doctor ordered. Other people simply experiencing the normal stresses of life can also experience a sense of profound relief in the "warm" embrace of a cult.

Ethics and the Modern Guru:

Does brainwashing cause specific (and perhaps irreversible) neural rewiring?

Benjamin Zablocki:

Yes, specific and no, not irreversible. We are still in the early stages of learning about such things as neuroplasticity and mirror neurons but we know enough to understand the elasticity of our brains even in adulthood can make us terribly vulnerable to victimhood, but wonderfully available to recovery. I think in the next 10 to 15 years, we will know a lot more about how to facilitate recovery, but even now, success rates are high if the victim wants to succeed and the environment is understanding and supportive. Most troublesome to erase are implanted false memories but that's another story for another time.

Ethics and the Modern Guru:

When it comes to the psychological mechanisms (and related brain activity) are there similarities between brainwashing and addiction?

Benjamin Zablocki:

Yes, but I would put it a little differently. I would say that brainwashing induces a new addiction, to the love and approval of the leader and/or the group. This addiction is a part of the brainwashing process but it's not the whole thing. Thinking of brainwashing solely as a form of addiction can be misleading because it ignores the equally important cognitive intellectual reprogramming involved in brainwashing.

Ethics and the Modern Guru:

Are the three phases of brainwashing (stripping—group identification—death/rebirth) linear, meaning that unless there is first a proper stripping etc. there can be no successful coercion?

Benjamin Zablocki:

That's one of the problems of behavioral science theories. In order to write about these things, we have to put them in a simplistic linear order. Reality is always messier and more variable. The earlier stages usually continue mixed in with the latter. Especially stripping and group identification can sometimes go round and round, each reinforcing the other.

Ethics and the Modern Guru:

Is everyone prone to being brainwashed? What can one do to protect oneself from it?

Benjamin Zablocki:

Yes, everyone is susceptible if we're unlucky or unwary enough to put ourselves in totalitarian isolated clutches. If you find yourself being isolated from previous social ties, you should run for the exit. It's true that some disciplines (like medical school or military service) can require a certain amount of isolation from your previous surroundings. But if you aren't even allowed to have an occasional phone conversation with a parent or a sibling or a devoted old friend, I'd be concerned.

Ethics and the Modern Guru:

If a full psycho-neurological model of brainwashing is possible, would this also mean that such a model could greatly aid in the recovery from the trauma associated with brainwashing?

Benjamin Zablocki:

We are still pretty far from a full psycho-neurological model of anything and most especially brainwashing. But, yes, the more we know, the better and easier recovery will be.

Ethics and the Modern Guru:

Since recovery from cults is (as you state) a washing of washing, does this mean these processes are irreversible? If so, does recovery come with its own kind of trauma?

Benjamin Zablocki:

The process is definitely NOT IRREVERSIBLE. This is important to emphasize because the victim can sometimes feel like the brain has been tied in such knots that it will never be able to be untied. This has not proven to be the case. That's why a fluid metaphor like washing is more appropriate than something like knotting or pounding. Supportive families of brainwashing victims have to understand that recovery from brainwashing is like recovery from trauma or traumatic abuse. It is asymptotic. That means it can go to 50% cured, then to 75%, then to 90%, then to 95%, then to 99%, then maybe to 99.9%. But never to 100%. One can recover from brainwashing, but one never escapes a certain fragility that was not there before and that just has to be lived with forever. But, with common sense and supportive friends and family, this need not prevent one from having a normal and happy life.

Ethics and the Modern Guru:

Can brainwashing cause mental illness (besides trauma)?

Benjamin Zablocki:

Like any trauma, brainwashing can tip a person over into a mental illness if the mental illness was already latent before the brainwashing. Practically, this means that a cure for a such a person will require treating both the brainwashing and the mental illness. Fortunately, there are organizations and therapists with training and experience in this area.

Ethics and the Modern Guru:

Strictly from a neurological point of view (when looking at the behavior of neurons and the release etc. of neurotransmitters) is there a difference between the activity occurring during brainwashing and taking certain drugs? Meaning, is the successful brainwashing a very specific process, involving very specific brain activity?

Benjamin Zablocki:

Drugs affecting oxytocin and natural opioids may be implicated. We really don't know very much about this. For what little is known, the question is best addressed to an M.D.

Ethics and the Modern Guru:

Is there any area of the brain that is more involved in the process of brainwashing than the others?

Benjamin Zablocki:

There's no simple answer to this question. Several different areas of the brain seem to be involved and I don't know enough about how they work together to feel confident about giving you a detailed answer to this question. Unfortunately, I'm not sure that anybody currently around would be able to answer this question. Ask it again in another ten years. research in this area is progressing rapidly. As we learn more, the answers will be coming less from social and behavioral scientists like myself and more from neuroscientists.

Ethics and the Modern Guru:

Can the trauma caused by brainwashing be fully healed? The "black holes", can they ever be integrated again within a healthy brain structure?

Benjamin Zablocki:

The black hole is a scary metaphor. But, yes, the prognosis seems to be favorable if the victim really wants to recover and is lucky enough to have supportive friends and family. Oh, and I should have said supportive and patient friends and family. I can't overemphasize the importance of patience. If you love a brainwashing victim, be prepared to have your patience torture tested. Just when you think everything is hunky-dory, there may be some backsliding. For the caregivers, it may be important to remember that you can love and support a brainwashing victim back to health (or so close to health that you won't notice the difference). But you will NEVER FULLY UNDERSTAND what the brainwashing victim went through and what she still has to go through to keep the tiny black holes from getting big again.

Ethics and the Modern Guru:

The danger of revisiting the guru etc., is this similar to the alcoholic getting a taste of alcohol again?

Benjamin Zablocki:

Well, kind of. But maybe more like a victim of battle-field trauma being suddenly exposed to fireworks going off.

Ethics and the Modern Guru:

Why are those the most resistant to brainwashing the slowest to recover?

Benjamin Zablocki:

This is a question I've thought about for a long time and I haven't found the answer. It kind of makes sense to me in a very vague sense and it is supported by clinical evidence. I think if we could really figure out the answer to this, we would be a lot further along at being able to help the victims, even the victims who don't want to be helped.

Ethics and the Modern Guru:

Is there anything one can do in order to safeguard oneself from brainwashing (and manipulation etc. in general)?

Benjamin Zablocki:

Beware of isolated environments with totalitarian control. Beware of ideologies that offer answers to all the world's problems. Beware of anyone or anything that asks you to cut all ties to previous loved ones or that makes you believe than none of them ever really cared about you.

program & error

by Steven Van Neste

-1-   Nothing is, perhaps, scarier than the idea of brainwashing; so much so that some even go as far as to deny there is such a thing. What brainwashing exactly is, seems rather difficult to answer, however, what should be inquired into first, is just as to why brainwashing is so frightening, as well as the more general topic of cults and cultish influences.

Some may liken the entire complex to a form of modern slavery, and though there is a definite truth to this, it also does not appear to be entirely accurate. The reason is that slavery is always, more or less, a corporeal event and in most cases is something that goes against the will; the fears of brainwashing and cultish influence, however, are precisely because they seem to infiltrate inside (and operates within) our concept of free will.

If we were to watch a movie involving slavery, then this usually will not translate into fear, because (at least in the Western Hemisphere) we have become accustomed to our liberal ways of life. Even more so, it is something that can be fought against; the best example of which is the Haitian slave revolution at the end of the 18th century. The fear of brainwashing is, however, more severe than this because it turns us into something worse than a slave.

The classical image of brainwashing victims (and often of cult members in general) is that of a zombie, and though many professionals would warn against this image, it must be understood, that this is how most will see the situation and hence why it is something so feared. Whether the zombie metaphor is accurate is beside the point, for the simple reason that to many this is exactly how it seems, and this is why we fear it the way we do.

What we fear above all is someone turning us into something other than ourselves. As such the fear of cultish influence is not just a fear of enslavement, but more importantly is a fear of finding our entire sense of self hijacked. Where the zombie metaphor fails, however, is that it tends to portray it all as something simplistic, especially since it tends to make us believe cult members in general are like brainless tools; this, however, is not the case, since the attack is usually never upon our intelligence, but as aforementioned upon our sense of self.

If cultish influence purposes a danger of enslavement, then it is on a deeper level than the one we are used to, as it involves not so much simple physical coercion, as rather it operates on a more grayish psycho-physical level. The aim of classical slavery was usually one of mere labor, as such it usually was a process restricted to physical aggression, and there was little care about the mind. In other words, in classical slavery, the masters did not care whether or not it was the slaves will to obey, whereas within the context of cultish influence, the mind is central to everything, as the cult demands not only a performing body, but more importantly demands a willing mind.

-2-   But what is a cult? We all seem to know what it means, yet proper definition always escapes us. In one of its simplest forms, a cult could be described as an organization imposing its will upon the individual, thusly alienating said individual from society. Looking at the classical image of the cult, the first part of this description seems rather accurate, however, the latter part is more problematic, since it relates more to communes than it does to cults as such.

Perhaps we should first of all look at the etymology of the word 'cult'. It comes from the Latin *cultus* and means adoration or care; it is derived from the verb *colō* which designates both to cultivate, to protect and to inhabit. (The word 'sect', on the other hand, is derived from the Latin verb *sequi,* meaning to follow.) Historically the word cult was used for certain rites of adoration within an already established religion and does not denote something sinister by itself. This current more menacing meaning of cult is something that arose closer to the middle of the 20th century, but really only became prominent around the same time as the hippie-movement began and the west became more and more flooded by new forms of spirituality and quasi philosophical outlooks, which often were seen as something damaging to the regular order of society.

Philosophically speaking, we could say that the current usage of the word 'cult' means that which goes against the accepted norms of society, to be more accurate, however, we should state that cults are what goes against the *nomos* of society. The reason for this, is that the Greek word *nomos* (which translates both as habit and law) denotes a much deeper complex, which in turns brings us back to the difficulty of the word 'cult' in its current usage. Sometimes when browsing for definitions of cult, you will find it mentioned as a group operating in or existing at the fringes of society. This is important, because it reveals this general etymological evolution of cult, from a more or less general adoration, to a marginal adoration.

But why should there be fear and controversy concerning marginal adoration, and why is there this transition from general to marginal, because of which cults become redefined as something dangerous? Numerous books have been written on cults and many groups dedicate all their efforts to it, yet the irony is that these individuals/groups often are in the fringes of it all themselves. The reason for this is that few ever seek to inquire concerning a bigger picture, and hence many fail to understand the nature of both cult and society, for the simple reason that they fail to understand the concept of *nomos*.

-3- What exists at the margins of society is always a part of society and hence it cannot ever be simply discarded without damaging society itself. The error many people make, is to imagine the marginal can just be scraped away and what will remain shall be an omnipresent cohesiveness. However, society cannot exist without its boundaries and hence the marginal cannot ever be scraped away; figuratively, the cohesiveness of the inner-city can exist solely because of the fringes surrounding it.

What must be examined now, first of all, is not the cult itself, but rather the reason as to why we are scared of cults. Why must there be an awareness, and what is the *real* point/agenda of this awareness? The error of many self-styled cult experts, is often that they are so busy looking to the outside, that they forget to look back inside society itself. There are dangerous and destructive cults out there, this is for sure, yet it is not as simple as that, and hence this should not be seen as an excuse to not inquire into our 'accepted' society.

People who fight against cults tend to have the mistaken belief that since cults exist in the margins, that they are nourished there as well, this however is simply not so. A cult may be born and exist at the fringes of society, but what nourishes it is always society itself. Looking at the most frightening image of them all, The Peoples Temple, we find its impetus was not at all to exist at the fringes of society, but rather to transform society. Cults often are formed not because they are against society as such, but rather because they wish for a different society, and if they move to the fringes, then this is only because there are irreconcilable differences between the two.

-4- Many people thinking about cults would imagine that a movement towards the fringes is always suspicious and results in either a brainwashed commune of zombies, or worse, a mass graveyard. What

most will fail to take note of however, is that such a movement is not at all a rare or even dangerous phenomenon. To understand this better, one must only look at the history of Christianity, which began as a small sect heavily persecuted because they went against the *nomos* of the Roman Empire and hence early Christians often lived at the margins of society. Cappadocia (region in Central Turkey) contains cave cities, where early Christians lived, secluded away from a society which did not accept them.

Later on Christianity not only became established, especially through the patronage of emperor Constantine, but became the one true faith through emperor Gratian. The latter was also instrumental in the persecution of all heresies, since the earlier Council of Nicaea had established what Christianity ought to be like. So the movement we have thus far, is a faith that had been pushed to the fringes, has nonetheless managed to allowed itself not just to become accepted, but to become the new *nomos*, and thus in turn now commands the whole of society and as a result everything else is pushed to the fringes. And perhaps this is one of the reasons why we fear cults, because we are afraid of our own *nomos* becoming displaced, afraid that we ourselves may become banished to the fringes.

This of course is not where the history of Christianity ends, as much later on we find a whole new schism beginning with Luther's 'ninety-five theses'. The exact history of events is not important here, what is important, however, is that once again it led to the idea of how society should be, and of others being pushed to the fringes. Here we should also remember the etymology of cult, from the Latin verb *colō*; one of the meanings of this word is to inhabit, and this is exactly what we see as history continues, as countries became defined through their chosen 'cult'.

There is of a course a lot more to it, as it was not just a matter of some countries becoming Protestant and others remaining Catholic; it, more importantly, became an issue of both tolerance/freedom and of secular politics. This latter idea of secularization led, however, to new problems, since suddenly certain groups felt threatened and sought to escape these new political orders. Some of these 'cults' removed themselves from what is established so much so, that they even crossed an entire ocean, in order to be able to live a life designated by their own *nomos*.

With this in mind, it is rather ironic to realize that for a large part the anti-cult movement is rooted in the USA, since the first settlers in the USA can be described as cultists wishing to walk away from established society and sought to build their own communes and live in isolation from mainstream society. It is also important we keep this in mind, because a group wishing to isolate themselves from society, does not necessarily indicate something dangerous or sinister. In other words, a marginal group is not necessarily dangerous, and much in the same way, just because something is established and is part of mainstream society, does not mean it is good.

-5- Understanding the history of it all is important, because only by looking at a bigger picture can we at least try and make some sense of it all. As such, we must not only focus on the concepts of cult and society, but on the anti-cult mindset as well and how it relates to both cult and society. As seen already, the current usage of the word 'cult' is a rather recent invention and its impetus is the sudden arrival of new forms of spirituality. The interesting twist here, is that this new definition is by and large an invention of the anti-cult movement; it is, obviously, not the case that what may be dubbed a cult is an invention of the anti-cult movement, however, this new paradigm of cults is.

We can draw a parallel here with the historicity of the witch-hunts, there is no doubt that there may have been people who could be called witches as they were drawn to magical pagan traditions, however, the concept of witchcraft used by the witch hunters was one of their own invention. I do not mean to imply here that cult awareness is a bad thing, and I definitely am not saying there are no dangerous cults out there. What I am saying, however, is that we ought to be careful not to trap ourselves in the pitfalls of our own prejudices and ignorance, especially since if we do not look at the greater picture, we only end up feeding into the cult or worse, becoming one ourselves.

-6-   So what is it we should be aware of? The most important thing here is that we must always keep our own prejudices in check. Secondly, we must be extremely vigilant not to succumb to paranoia. With this in mind, it ought to be noted that a lot of cult awareness seems to be analogous to McCarthyism, this is also interesting, since theories of brainwashing were first developed in the USA's fight against Communism.

The rise of cult awareness goes together with the influx of new forms of spirituality (commonly referred to as new religious movements). Now, regardless of whether or not some of these new movements are indeed dangerous, we must first of all be daring to ask a few more important questions, namely, (1) why do people seek out these new forms, and (2) why do we feel threatened by this? That some of these new forms of spirituality are dangerous is irrelevant, because if we must be 'aware' of everything new and different, then we merely succumb to paranoia, so if we wish to learn, then we must first of all be willing to suspend our judgements.

More important is that we must be careful not to betray our own values and ideals, for if we say we wish to combat cults because they rob people of their freedom etc., then we must practice extreme care and ensure we ourselves do not impose our will upon others, thereby denying them their freedom. To understand this, we may look at McCarthyism, and how it black listed writers and artists because they had views that could be seen as communist and more generally were seen as un-American. All of this, in spite of the USA's first amendment, which declares for there to be freedom of speech.

Though cults are a global phenomenon, the anti-cult phenomenon is largely an American invention, and as such it should come as no surprise that often it is driven by a 'pathological' over-attachment to American values and ideals. As it seems, prominent anti-cult people often are driven not so much by a sense of care for others, as much rather they are driven by a desire to protect their own values. As such, concerning the inquiry as to why we fear cults, it appears that what often is the case; is that we feel the need to be aware of cults because we feel they infiltrate upon our own values and beliefs. The mistake of many cult experts, as such, is that their study is in the light of their own ideology, rather than being based upon mere facts. (Though of course, there is a greater problematic here, whether or not in such studies there can be neutral facts to begin with.)

As such, we must also be weary of possible hypocrisy, where we lambast the cult because it robs one of freedom, yet at the same time we often demand things to be a set in a certain way. In other words, we must always be careful to not just imprison the concept of freedom, and to allow the other the views he feels comfortable with. So always we must ask ourselves the question, whether or not the other's view is indeed dangerous or if it is just that we merely are uncomfortable with it because it goes against our own beliefs, opinions etc. There is a very fine line here, and always it is very easy to fall prey to hypocrisy, paranoia and a nauseating sense of overbearing self-certainty, by which we think that because something makes sense to me, thus it must make sense to the other.

-7-   Let us return now to the questions stated above, why do we (1) seek alternative forms and why do we (2) feel threatened by alternative forms? As we do this, however, we first of all must look into the concepts of the individual self and society.

In spite of our love for free will (and the subsequent fear of cultish influence and brainwashing etc.) what really defines both man and society is habitual neediness. To understand this, we must only look on the intermediate psychological level of what makes up one's individual self, and what we find here is that what makes us who we are is our habituality. Existentialist thought has rightfully sought to question this, yet has not accomplished much, for the simple reason that it is not just our own sense of self that it intrinsically linked to our own habits, but our own habits are also instrumental in the other's perception of our own self.

In other words, our sense of self is not at all some strange transcendental something, but relies heavily on whatever is habitual, more philosophically, we could state that the self is our personal *nomos*, the habits by which we become a 'lawful' entity. And what is society of course, if not a collection of individuals? Granted there may be a synergistic something to society, yet this does not imply that the principles governing it are any different than those governing the individual.

So beginning with the second question, the reason we feel threatened by alternative forms is because it is imagined these forms impose both upon the habits of our own self and those of society as a whole. The cult (in a more general sense of the word) is that which imposes upon the regular organization of society and hence we are weary of it because ultimately it seems to detract from our sense of self. There is of course a strange sense of hierarchy here, since why should my own sense of self be threatened by what goes against society? This, however, is not an easy question to answer, but suffice to say that our sense of self always greatly depends upon the presence of others, and hence it should come as no surprise that though society comes after the individual, that it does not take much and long, for the individual to become subservient to society.

The difficulty concerning this problematic, wherein our own individual self seems to be enslaved to society is where we find clues to answering our first question, since the reason why we seek alternative forms is because our own sense of self (our own habituality) finds itself oppressed by the habits of a society, that not before long starts to appear as something alien.

-8-   One of the reasons why the entire topic of cults and cultish influence is so complicated is because it is not something that is isolated to fringe groups, but is something encountered through the whole of society on every level imaginable. Our society is highly driven by consumerism, and the way this operates has a lot in common with cultism, so much so even, that some companies become almost like a cult. At first this may seem rather ridiculous, but that is only because we have not thought deep enough about it.

Just as we like to imagine we have free will (whether we do or not is not important here), we also like to imagine we think for ourselves and as such, the reason why we fear cults is not only because they force their will upon us, but also because they tell us what (and how) to think. What is almost forgotten, however, is that the whole of our society always forces itself upon us in pretty much the same manner. This is all the more so in our era of consumerist culture, where we are constantly bombarded by all sorts of thoughts and slogans.

Keeping the above in mind, it also should come as no surprise that cults operate in pretty much the same way as society itself does, and that its rhetoric and operational framework is not anything different from the rest of society. For instance, one of the complaints of cults is that how they canvass people by preying upon certain groups and/or weaknesses, however, in essence this is not any different from the way regular companies and institutions operate. As such, we cannot truly say that deception is a feature of cult, since it is not at all uncommon in ordinary society. Another example is how some cults will target university students or even high school kids, however, that they target specific groups is not at all unique, as it is common everywhere.

-9-   What must be understood, is that a cult is not at all that different from mainstream society and, hence, its lure is not at all something that mysterious. It is true that ignorance and naivety may be a leading cause of cult indoctrination, and in today's landscape saturated with new ageisms and spiritual junk, you do realize that sometimes it is a matter of gullibility and lesser intelligence, for the simple reason that some beliefs are just so out there that it does not take a lot of education to see through it.

The main reason people fall for cults, however, is not because they are prey to some outlandish belief, but rather because there is a dynamic similar to that of society, and because the cult offers a connection seemingly more genuine than what society has to offer. So except for some cases, most people fall prey to cults because of an emotional connection rather than because they feel a need to believe in something different. As such, the answer to the first question (as to why we seek alternative forms) is because it is not so much the content of the form that matters, but rather the way this form connects to our own self.

-10-   What most seek above all is not so much truth or comfort, but much rather connection. Perhaps because 'being' itself always appears as something mysterious and unattainable, we are led towards the desire to belong. As such, it is not so much that people are drawn to something different, as instead they seek something that is perceived as having become lost in society. Even if we look at The Peoples Temple and the reason why it was successful, we will find this was because it offered a renewed sense of belonging, and the people in it did not seek something radically different, but sought what they thought society ought to be like to begin with.

With this in mind, it is also interesting to note, that the two questions, (why we seek and why we fear) are very much intertwined, especially because depending on where you stand, it is always the other that is the cult. To he in mainstream society, the cult is a cult, but to he inside the cult, it is society which appears as a cult. Now, anti-cult people might be quick to jump to the conclusion this is because such is the way cults operate (by turning things the other way around etc.) and though there is a partial truth to this, it is far from the whole picture.

The manner whereby some fear cults is identical to the way some who are drawn to cults, are fearful of society, and just as some talk about the deceptions of cults, others talk about the deceptions of mainstream society, so it is far from a simple affair and is definitely not as straight cut as some would like to believe. It is all too easy to declare something as bad or dangerous, but much harder to actively try and understand it, and it is even easier to see something as cultish, while failing to realize our own society shares many of those same characteristics.

Added to this, is the potential danger of anti-cultism becoming cult-like itself, as such regardless of perceived danger, one must always inquire beyond the appearance of it all, and as mentioned already, one must keep his own prejudices etc. in check. It is indeed good to be weary of and cultivate an awareness against cults attempting to rob individuals of their freedom, but we must always be careful that we ourselves do not impose our will upon the other, thereby denying him his freedom.

It is good to create cult awareness, and one should never go to the other extreme and fail to see there is a reality to cults that can be dangerous. There are groups out there and we should be watchful of them, just as there are unhealthy beliefs and practices which ought not to be encouraged. In others words, there is this fine line and if one wishes to cultivate genuine information and awareness, then one always ought to be mindful of this, because it is very easy to just fall into the trap of being a self-styled cult expert who deems everything cultish except for his own beliefs.

-11-   Concerning this ever present danger of hypocrisy, it ought to be mentioned that a lot of anti-cultism is rooted in 'mainstream' religion (especially Evangelical Christianity) and a need to stand up for the idea of certain accepted values, so in the USA you will find some who consider everything a cult that promotes things alien to traditional American values, and likewise, you will find groups who have conferences including a strong Christian agenda. This is all the more interesting and important, when we consider the climate (touched upon earlier) in which ant-cultism was born and the controversy concerning the 'scene' of deprogramming.

The climate in which anti-cultism was born is one of a general paranoia not just towards anything new, but also towards anything that was different from the norms and habits of American Christianity, it should come as no surprise that 'satanic panic' arose around the same time. It is also important to understand that anti-cultism is not just directed against groups belonging to a faith different than Christianity, but is also directed against any Christian-based group which also has teachings radically different from what is accepted by the main Evangelical bodies.

Suffice to say that the main impetus of the deprogramming scene and the many different networks of cult awareness is one of self-righteousness rather than actual care or concern. This becomes even more obvious when we look at the methods employed by deprogrammers which involved not just brainwashing techniques, but also actively kidnapping people, holding them against their will and instances of sexual assault. Regardless of whether or not deprogrammers rescued people from dangerous cults, the way they operate is often of questionable ethics and, possibly, dangerous to the psyche of the victim.

In essence deprogramming is identical to brainwashing, and even if it is done for the right reasons, we will find it is akin to exorcism, where a mental problem is only made worse through the use of coercive techniques. The brainwashing techniques involved are not of a passive kind, but involve an active breaking of the psyche through the use of discipline and sleep deprivation, in other words, torture with the aim of reforming thought.

Of course, one may argue that if a person was truly trapped in a dangerous cult and now he is out and 'free', then where lies the harm? This however is a dangerously ignorant way of thinking, since what has been reformed is never thought itself, since what takes place in actuality is physical change within the brain. The brain does of course enjoy a high degree of plasticity and alters itself constantly, but then, we must be mindful and not overstate this fact, for just as the physical body in general has a great ability to heal itself, we would not say it is a good thing that therefore we can just injure the body and expect no consequences.

-12-   In spite of its plasticity, the brain is also a highly vulnerable organ which prefers to work in a more or less uniform manner, as such the change that occurs through brainwashing (which includes deprogramming) is not something 'natural' but is the result of trauma.

Especially the early scene of deprogramming was (for the most part) one of renegades operating out of sense of ideology rather than genuine psychological concern, as such there often was little concern over the psycho-neurological reality of what went on.

The brainwashing's metaphor of fluidity should never be taken too literal, for though it has been shown that people can be brainwashed by a cult and then 'brainwashed' again through a deprogrammer, we should not come to think that minds can just be changed like that without consequence. One set of thoughts being replaced by another is never just a mental event, but always is a neurological event as well, so in other words, it is 'physical' as much as it is psychological. More importantly, neurological processes are never simple and hence it is not just a matter of something new being written on the mind's blackboard.

Though people can certainly come back from being brainwashed, it is rather doubtful one can ever be fully 'normal' again, since it seems there shall always be some sort of a psychological scar tissue. Since brainwashing relies heavily on creating trauma, it should be obvious why deprogramming is rather unhealthy, since ultimately it will create a greater trauma, hence the real need is to understand better both the science of brainwashing and the entire complex of cults and cultish influences. As such, it should also be understood that the idea of deprogramming is largely in error, since in effect it is always a re-programming.

-13-   As stressed multiple times already, it is greatly important one always keeps his own prejudices in check, since quite a few people came to be anti-cult activists because they themselves had been the victim of a cult, as such, we must be careful never to project our own victimhood in the situation. When driven to aid someone, our approach

should not be one of force, but one of genuine care whereby we seek to understand the other's motivations and work from there.

As mentioned above, the idea of deprogramming is in error because in reality it always is a re-programming, and it is important this is really understood, because all of us always are programmed. All of our actions, our thoughts, beliefs and opinions, whether they are of our own design or not, are always programmed inside of us. With this in mind, it is also interesting to reflect on the origin of the term brainwashing, which is a loan translation from the Chinese xǐnǎo, which was popularized by the Communist Party and was widely used by chairman Mao.

This 'etymology' of the word 'brainwashing is of great interest because it comes to show many things that are quite different from its usual association with cults living at the fringes of society. Brainwashing was an important aspect of Mao's revolution, because it was the final tool in his process of re-education. To understand this better, we must look at the whole of what was meant by re-education, since the idea here was not so much to offer a new and revolutionary way of thinking, but rather to undo what was considered the decadence of Western influence. Brainwashing, as such, was meant rather literally, as a washing away of the crud of Western decadence.

Chairman Mao certainly would have defended the use of brainwashing as a vital process to remove undue influence, as such we could say he encouraged 'deprogramming', because he felt it allowed people to return to the 'normalcy' of Chinese society, and he would suggest that it is the Western decadent who is 'brainwashed'. Perspective must always be kept in mind, not because we want to white wash things, but because it is necessary in order to see the bigger picture. It is of course tempting to imagine the fight between Communism and the West as one of good versus evil, but that is just to fall back into myth and ignorance, for what really took place is a fight between two ideologies, each of which asserting itself as the one true way.

So returning to an earlier theme, what we had in the fight between the West and Communism, was a collision between two radically different instances of *nomos* (habit), and regardless of whether one is better or not, both always are guilty of cult-like indoctrination and wish to program people according to their version of *nomos*. As such, in examining a cult the first question that must be asked is, whether or not my suspicion is because I care about the supposed victim, or if I am just being led by the habits of my own environment.

-14-   It is said, that one of the dangers of brainwashing is how the subject has the impression of acting out of his own free will; this, however, is not just the case for brainwashing but for the entirety of cultish influence, since even a regular cult member will not think he is just there because he fell for propaganda.

The issue of free will is difficult because it is wholly philosophical and is even more problematic than that of consciousness, suffice to say that hence it should come as no surprise it is always the other who lacks free will, whereas our own self is always certain to be free. The problem of free will is furthermore complicated because it is a conglomerate of two ideas (freedom and will) which taken by themselves already present us with enormous difficulties, as it is obvious we are threading in dangerous waters and a complete 'answer' may not ever be found.

The question always ought to be kept in mind is: how do I know I am acting out of my own free will? As stated already, a lot of cult awareness people act from within the bias of their own society, so they talk about others being deceived and having their free will taken away, yet they themselves might be acting as such, merely because they are the victim of a society they take for granted. This of course is a double edged sword, since it also applies to those seeking 'alternative forms', because often it does not take much for a more general suspicion of mainstream society to turn into something gullible, whereby the alternative is immediately taken for granted.

-15-   It is not so much that cults are everywhere, but rather it is that everywhere we always are trapped inside of them already. Whether there is free will or not, how can we ever know anything? As mentioned earlier, the rise of anti-cultism was largely due to the influence of certain values taken for granted; but where do these values come from and how do they differ from other values? In short, we are quick to judge because we are trapped within our own personal cult of habit, and failing to see these habits are partially due to the outside world, we come to imagine that anything different from our own habits must be abnormal.

Complacency is often dangerous and must be guarded against, as such we should learn to always keep up our defenses and be motivated to inquire concern the bigger picture. It is the lack of such inquiry that leaves one most vulnerable to cultish influence, be it in the form of actual cult indoctrination or the many forms of propaganda found throughout mainstream society. It must also be understood that values do not exist as absolutes and that it is easy for us to compromise our own values because of certain circumstances.

The concept of the exception does not just belong to the socio-political realm, but also has its place within the psychology of the individual. If we are opposed to cults because they rob one of his freedom, then how can we justify forcing someone out of a cult? To many people within cult awareness this will sound like a naïve question, yet it only betrays a naivety present within their own minds, because they refuse to inquire and hence fall prey to something indoctrinated in them through their own habituality. It is very tempting to state that the cult is evil, but this is also incredibly cheap and naïve, for what is evil?

If we wish for there to be genuine awareness, then we should not be stooping to the level of mythology and divide things into good and evil, because these are merely labels we use for our own benefit. It is always our own values which are good and the other ones who are evil, as such, someone trapped in a cult does not think or feel he is in something evil, no, the cultist sees the cult as good and the rest of the world as evil. So we must be aware of such mythologies, especially since dividing things into good and evil is one of the ways cults operate.

-16-   Understanding all of the above is all the more important if one ever wishes to understand and help those who have fallen prey to a cult. The days of deprogramming are largely behind us now, as it has been replaced by the idea of 'exit counseling', however, a change of methodology does not necessarily mean a change in understanding. The question to be asked is simple: are we forcing the person out of the cult through manipulation, or are we guiding him to come to his own decisions? It is very easy to say one is free to his own mind, it is a whole another matter though, to actually grant the other said freedom of mind.

Another question, what happens to the person after the exit? Are we guiding the person towards his own individuality, or are we forcing him to be a part of our own society? Do we force upon him our own values, or do we guide him to discover his own? Such questions are of course hard and since they mainly belong to philosophy, it is hard (if not impossible) to find real (let along definite) answers. However, that a question is philosophical is not at all an excuse to not ask it, especially since in every society ethics is always important, and ethics is always the domain of philosophy.

More importantly, as mentioned already, all our thoughts are always physical events as well as mental events, since they are the result of neurological activity. As such, what should be done in aiding cult victims is not so much an attempt to replace thoughts, but rather an attempt to heal by encouraging active thinking. The way brainwashing works is by as much as possible disabling one's ability to think; mainstream manipulations as well wish for you to not think, and though they do not physically interfere with you, they do use certain techniques to discourage thinking. To understand this better, one must only look at politics and its rhetoric, which tends to use easy images invoking a feeling of mythology, this is so, because rhetoric always concerns the invocation of emotions through the presentation of images rather than facts.

-17-   If we merely force our own values upon a cult victim then we cannot possibly say that we have cured that person. If all we do is replace one set of thoughts with another, then we have not accomplished anything and regardless of whether or not the supposed victim is now in a better situation, we have not achieved anything other than manipulating another's mind. Perhaps the person really was the victim of a destructive cult and we may have very well saved that person from harm, but we cannot ever say that we have cured that person.

As stated above, all forms of manipulation and cultish influence operate by limiting the activity of thinking (brainwashing and deprogramming are only the worst of this since they involve direct physical coercion techniques). One of the ways this occurs in the brain is by shutting down neural connections and causing shorter routes of action. When it comes to the marvels of the brain, we tend to be enamored by the grey matter (see for instance Agatha Christie's famous detective Hercule Poirot), though the underlying white matter is just as important.

In a rather simplified manner we could say that whereas the thoughts are stored in the grey matter, thinking relies heavily on white matter, because thinking involves connections and white matter is mainly made up out of axons rather than nerve cell bodies. As such, what occurs in different forms of manipulation often goes together with a decrease in the activity inside the white matter, leading to a lessened activity of thinking. A real healing of someone who has been the victim of a cult should be one that stimulates thinking and hence leads to an increase in neuronal activity by forging more connections. With this in mind, it is also of interest to note, that people who already think more, tend to have a greater number of interconnecting neurons and are usually more defended against cultish influence.

-18-   To end with, I would like to refer to (and build upon) a book by Robert Lifton entitled 'The Protean Self' which is, for the most part, a celebration of a multi-faceted psyche. The greatest strength by which we may deal with an ever changing world, is by having a self that has many faces, rather than being restricted to a singular mask.

The best defense against cultish influence is not by going on countless anti-cult tirades, but by allowing ourselves to cultivate such a Protean self as described by Lifton; this can be achieved by learning about the world and by allowing ourselves to think things through rather than rely on ready-made opinions. We should always ask the question: is this really what I think? Relying on cheap mythologies of good versus evil, proper democratic values, Christian morality etc., does not solve anything but only contributes to the problem.

What we should be aware of is not so much cults but rather our own self and the way we stand within and interact with society, as such we should cultivate a strong sense of self-individuality/responsibility. This also means that we must learn to be tolerant and respect what is other, especially since this will allow us to better judge whether something is dangerous or not, since we will be less trapped in mythologies. It must also be understood, that a strong sense of self does not mean one should succumb to deliberate eccentricity or an otherwise overbearing sense of self.

In other words, cultivating a sense of self does not mean we reduce ourselves to the fate of a loner or social outcast. The Protean self is not someone who fears society and hence needs to withdraw from it, to the contrary, because his self is multi-faceted he can move through society with ease, because he is not bothered by the face of alterity. The idea of the Protean self is also not to be confused with Ronald Laing's divided self. The divided self occurs when the sense of self is not strong enough to deal with different streams, the answer to this problematic is either to become trapped in a mythological self or to fall a victim to mental illness. The Protean self, on the other hand, protects itself from such division by allowing to move in a bigger picture and live in a much larger world than a self that operates on a basis of division.

In conclusion, it is of great interest to note that just as brainwashing involves a metaphor of fluidity, so does the idea of the Protean self, since Proteus is a sea deity. The Protean self protects us because we become fluid and hence less susceptible to 'washings' because it is a self that is not defined through thoughts but through thinking. How we can open ourselves up to such a thing is of course not something easy, since unlike what is offered by cults, coaches, gurus etc., the Protean self is not a 'ware' that can be given through courses or teachings. Education is, of course, always a great aid towards a building of rationality and versatility, yet by itself does not guarantee anything, since unless we are actively thinking for ourselves education will just be a play of thoughts and memory. Finally, as was stressed by the mathematician George Polya, the way to teach is not by giving the problem followed by the answer, no, the way to teach is by stating the problem and offer just enough clues so that one may find the solution by one's own power of reasoning.

-19-   To summarize, if we lament that cults indoctrinate the individual and takes away his liberty, then we must first of all ensure that we are not guilty of the same. Furthermore, we must be careful so as not to confuse exotic sounding beliefs with something dangerous; likewise, we should not be blind to our own odd beliefs. What is also important to keep in mind, is that cults are not necessarily spiritual. Everything has the potential to be a cult, even atheist groups claiming to be against spirituality. Even the promise of a thinking that shall end all fear and set you free etc. is a perfect cult setup, because the grammar of 'to think' is rather confusing. To this we add all sorts of life coaches and self-management groups, which all tend to convince the individual that there is this correct way of 'thinking' and 'being', that shall make you successful and superior. Cults and undue influence are a socio-psychological phenomenon and the way to safeguard ourselves against it is through education, inquiry and introspection. Too often we fall into an us versus them mentality and trap ourselves in a rhetoric of hate, whereby everything else is stupid and we alone stand at the summit of reason and think clearly. This however, only leads to greater blindness, as it means we close of our minds to the actuality of cults and undue influence. The best protection against cults, besides education etc., is to always be aware of our humanity and its fragility. Everyone can fall, and failure to realize this only brings us one step closer towards delusion.

notes on critical thinking

One of the strangest features of our human consciousness is that always it is taken for granted, which is in part one of the marvels of our brain, namely that it always presents everything as a whole; so, for instance, we never perceive as if the world ends at the edges of our visual field, or when we look at something and then cover one eye, we do not feel as if half our vision has disappeared. Consciousness always appears as whole and perfect, and more importantly it always appears as mine. An added effect of this, is that likewise our thinking always appears as our own, as do our thoughts and memories.

We always take for granted that our thinking is our own, and that our thoughts and beliefs are our own, yet more often than not we are not willing to inquire into our cognitions and hence we become vulnerable to manipulations. Thinking is always taken for granted and precisely therein lies the problem, as more often than not we merely imagine we are thinking, as we have never learned to really think. Part of the problem, of course, is the odd grammar of 'to think'. To a certain extent we of course all think, since every process of cognition is in fact dependent on thinking, so if you are asked what you want for dinner, the answer you give is a result of thinking. Even more so, a person who has been brainwashed is still a thinking person, and even if I am asked a question and answer without thinking about it, the answer I give still is a result of thinking.

Needless to say that entire volumes can be written about the oddity of thinking, most of which is not a concern for now. What is a concern, however, is this deeper aspect of thinking which may referred to as critical thinking. What is meant here is a stricter grammar, as such, critical thinking is not so much concerned with the regular cognitive definition of thinking, but rather it is concerned with a certain 'rightness' of thinking.

Of course, herein we already find another problem, as it would be easy to misconstrue the meaning of said 'rightness'. To clarify this further, it ought to be noted that the word 'critical' is derived from the Greek *kritikós*, which means 'to judge'; the proper meaning of critical thinking is, as such, a thinking through which one may judge properly.

So critical thinking is an epistemological issue and hence correct thinking is not that much concerned with the actual validity of thoughts, but rather with the act of thinking itself, its structure etc. What is meant, hence, with rightness of thinking, is solely whether the thinking leads to proper judgement and revelation, or if it causes things to remain hidden. It is important to understand this, because we should always be weary of people who try to teach us proper thinking apart from critical thinking, because proper rationality is not so much something that concerns content but rather form.

Critical thinking is of vital importance in safeguarding ourselves from manipulation, as basically it is what allows us to see 'through' thinking, in other words, critical thinking is the thinking whereby we inquire into thinking and learn to analyze things in a formal and cohesive manner. One of the first aspects to be aware of, is how one must discern between premises and conclusions, this is especially important because often we fall prey to things because we buy into conclusions even in the absence of real premises. Proper thinking is not concerned with mere verbosity, in other words, it is not just a collection of statements, but an organized whole whereby conclusions follow naturally from premises through a proper logical syntax.

The other significant aspect, is that we must always be weary of the difference between deductive and inductive reasoning; the former concerns strictly abstract ideas and hence is mainly mathematical in nature, whereas the latter concerns our physical world and the 'facts' it contains. The main importance of this difference concerns the limits of reason. Deductive reason, as such, is always valid, so "1+1=2" is always true and can never be otherwise, but there is no such absolutism for inductive reason. "When the sky darkens it shall rain", does not have to be true; even if yesterday it was fact that the sky darkened and then it was fact that it began raining, does not mean there is a necessary connection. As such, it is important that the use of 'facts' in inductive reasoning is properly understood, because what is meant by the word is something isolated in time. That something is a fact now, does not necessarily mean it shall be so tomorrow.

The limits posed upon inductive reasoning must always be kept in mind, since for the most part our thinking tends to be concerning the world of facts, and even when we think of more abstract ideas such as society, we are still within the realm of inductive reason, and hence all problems concerning how we ought to live, behave, 'think' etc., cannot ever be solved in an absolute manner, because it is rooted in a world of transience. The extra obstacle in inductive reasoning is, hence, that it is not just a matter of proper logical form, but also a matter of inquiring into the soundness of the premises.

Understanding the problematic of inductive reason, we must also ensure that we do not fall into the other trap, namely radical relativism. That facts are not absolute does not mean that we cannot use them to form a coherent picture of our world. So the first thing we must inquire into, is whether or not something is a fact indeed, or if instead it is perhaps fantasy; such an inquiry allows us to cut away what is superstition. To this we add the stability of the fact, in other words: How often has the fact occurred? Does it always occur as such? Etc. Thirdly, we must also inquire into the fact and attempt to make sense of it, it is here we find the importance of scientific method, as it allows us to move further within proper inductive reasoning and hence leads us towards an understanding of the fact, so that we may better judge by it.

www.ingramcontent.com/pod-product-compliance
Lightning Source LLC
Chambersburg PA
CBHW050505290526
45786CB00006B/2438